SAYONARA, MICHELANGELO

Addison-Wesley Publishing Company, Inc.

Reading, Massachusetts   Menlo Park, California
New York   Don Mills, Ontario   Wokingham, England
Amsterdam   Bonn   Sydney   Singapore   Tokyo   Madrid
San Juan   Paris   Seoul   Milan
Mexico City   Taipei

SAYONARA MICHELANGELO

The Sistine Chapel Restored and Repackaged

Waldemar Januszczak

All acknowledgments for permission to reprint previously published material can be found on page 208.

Many of the designations used by manufacturers and sellers to distinguish their products are claimed as trademarks. Where those designations appear in this book and Addison-Wesley was aware of a trademark claim, the designations have been printed in initial capital letters (i.e., Gaines Cat Food).

Library of Congress Cataloging-in-Publication Data

Januszczak, Waldemar.
    Sayonara, Michelangelo : the Sistine Chapel restored and repackaged / Waldemar Januszczak.
        p.   cm.
    ISBN 0-201-52395-7
    ISBN 0-201-56750-4 (pbk.)
    1. Mural painting and decoration, Italian—Conservation and restoration—Vatican City. 2. Mural painting and decoration, Renaissance—Conservation and restoration—Vatican City. 3. Sistine Chapel (Vatican Palace, Vatican City) 4. Michelangelo Buonarroti, 1475–1564—Criticism and interpretation. I. Title.
ND2757.V35J3 1990
759.5—dc20   90-34331

Jacket & text design by Copenhaver Cumpston
Set in 11½-point Garamond #3 by DEKR Corporation, Woburn, MA
Display type is Lithos, designed by Carol Twombly at Adobe Systems, Inc.

Jacket photo, detail from "The Creation of Adam," courtesy of the Vatican Museum.
1 2 3 4 5 6 7 8 9-MW-9594939291
First printing, August 1990
First paperback printing, July 1991

FOR YUMI, AS ALWAYS

CONTENTS

MICHELANGELO/CHARLTON HESTON:
   "It's only painted plaster, Holy Father."

JULIUS II/REX HARRISON:
   "No, my son. It's much more than that. Much more."

Michelangelo was thirty-three when he began his involvement with the Sistine Chapel. He was sixty-six when he ended it. Those are the kinds of figures that can make an observer superstitious.

There has been much fanciful speculation about why the Sistine ceiling was painted. There has been much fanciful speculation about almost everything connected with Michelangelo. He is an artist who long ago achieved the large but indistinct outline of a mythological hero. "God! What a man! What beauty!" gasped Delacroix in his Journal of 1824. Sir Joshua Reynolds in his retirement speech as president of the Royal Academy in London insisted: "I should desire that the last words which I should pronounce in this

Academy . . . might be the name of Michael Angelo."

This book has been written on the premise that if you stop closing your eyes and feeling Reynolds-like awe in the presence of Michelangelo and start opening your eyes and feeling puzzled, by him, his work, his libido, you will *not* experience a lower class of enlightenment. On the contrary. The restoration of the Sistine ceiling that took place throughout most of the 1980s was an opportunity for more people to get closer to Michelangelo than ever before. It was an opportunity for many of us to peer through the Nietzschean mists that have swirled about him for so long and actually touch his handiwork. For the first time in nearly five hundred years, access to Michelangelo's masterpiece was public enough for the restorer's scaffolding to be crowded. Every time I went up that rickety ladder I found scores of others who had climbed it before me. Everyone, I noticed, was sneakily stroking the fresco when the restorer's backs were turned. I am sure that all of us climbed back down again feeling that we had finally managed to come close enough to Michelangelo to enjoy—and vouch for—his humanity.

If the French historian Jules Michelet had been as close to the Sistine ceiling as I and thousands of others have been he could never have written his famously silly assertion that when Michelangelo embarked upon this great fresco he had never before picked up a brush. According to Michelet, the painter of the Sistine Chapel sprang—like Eve out of Adam's side—fully formed into the world. The fact that the restorers have actually found grubby hog's hair bristles embedded in the paintwork seems in itself a refutation of this fantastic claim. Michelangelo, up close, is palpably a worker. He pummels his hog's hair brush. He eradicates mistakes. He takes shortcuts. He repeats himself. And in my book (this book) his achievement in painting the Sistine Chapel is greater for it.

The 1980s restoration campaign finally put an end to all the fanciful speculation as to why the Sistine ceiling was painted and made clear that the fresco was embarked upon for splendidly realistic reasons. The restorer's observations confirmed what Vatican records had revealed, that in the spring of 1504 there had been a massive structural collapse in the great chapel which Sixtus IV, "an old man in a hurry," had thrown up in such an un-Renaissance haste between 1477 and 1483. The collapse in the structure of the Sistine Chapel in 1504 caused a great crack to appear in the ceiling. This was the most important chapel in Christendom: it had to be repaired. Sixtus' nephew, Julius II, who owed his entire religious career to his uncle's nepotistic largesse, must have decided almost immediately that the roof should be restored and that the existing ceiling, a blue one decorated with a galaxy of twinkling silver stars, must be replaced.

According to Michelangelo's friend Piero Roselli, writing home to Florence on May 10, 1506, in the earliest known document relating to Michelangelo's involvement in the project, the pope's architect, Bramante, had counseled Julius II not to entrust Michelangelo with the Sistine ceiling commission: "Holy Father, I believe that Michelangelo would lack the necessary courage to attack the ceiling because he has not had much experience in figure painting, and in general the figures will be set high and in foreshortening."

Between July, 1508, when Michelangelo hired five assistants to help in the painting, and October 31, 1512, when the entire fresco was unveiled, young Buonarroti in fact succeeded in including three hundred and thirty-six assorted figures on the Sistine ceiling. Three hundred thirty-five and one-half of these still remain; in 1797 an explosion of gunpowder in the nearby Castel Sant' Angelo caused a large slab of paintwork containing most of a male nude to fall off. A head and two feet are all that survive of the Sistine's twentieth *ignudo.* Having painted three hundred and thirty-six figures on the roof Michelangelo went on, during his second Sistine fresco campaign, from 1536 to 1541, to accommodate another four hundred and thirteen figures in the Last Judgement that he painted on the altar wall. Altogether he and his assistants covered nearly ten thousand square feet of ceiling and over two thousand square feet of Last Judgement. Bramante was proved seriously wrong.

Teibi Katayama exists. He is my father-in-law. Hiroko exists. For forty years she has been warming Teibi's *sake* for him when he comes home in the evenings. If either of them knew what liberties I was taking with their basic identities they might be annoyed. Luckily neither of them speaks English.

On my visits to the Sistine scaffolding the three wise Vatican restorers, Signors Colalucci, Rossi, and Bonetti, were unflinchingly helpful and patient. Fabrizio Mancinelli told me some exciting things. A climb onto the scaffold with Pat Rubin was particularly enlightening. Helen Oldfield did what she always does: she sent me. Martha Moutray edited me back to some semblance of reality when I too grew too fanciful.

were until eighth, behind and patient. behind when
... ... for some exciting things, ... think ... ...
... with the Aubusson, ...
Note Office did what the answer ... ...
Maybe Monsieur asked the help to have touched ...
politician Bonaparte too careful.

It's a few seconds before 10 A.M. on a cool Tokyo morning in January, 1989. Hiroko Katayama switches off the microwave in which she has been heating up some water for *ocha* and looks up at her television. She's watching NTV—the Nippon Television Network Corporation—and the commercials are on. There's a jingle for Bon Curry—*Ooohhh. Aaahhh. You can smell it!* And a new refrigerator that delivers hundreds of perfectly formed ice cubes at the touch of a senso-button, promised by Toshiba. Then a tune Hiroko finds vaguely familiar drifts slowly across a perfect woodland scene, with conifers and a rushing stream. The camera stops at a fat white cat curled up like a puffball in the shade. Hiroko recognizes the tune. It's "Beautiful

Dreamer." A voice interrupts her own beautiful dreams—
Gaines Cat Food. Aaahhh. Ooohhh.

The clock that ticks eternally in the corner of the
breakfast screen informs Hiroko that it is 10 A.M. exactly.
And the NTV logo duly appears before her, magically
assembled from all sorts of curious computerized frag-
ments, city skyscrapers, baseball diamonds, cute cartoon
characters, they have all played their part in making NTV
what it is today. To celebrate the company's thirty-five
years of success, the logo tells her, NTV now presents a
special anniversary program. Hiroko has never been to
Rome so she does not immediately recognize the famous
melon-shaped outline of Michelangelo's dome for St. Peter's basilica that now emerges, shimmering, above her
television's horizon. (If the truth be told, she has not until
this fateful morning even heard of Michelangelo.) But
gorgeous sunrises are the same the world over. They fill
the sky with liquid gold and they fill the soul with hope.
We appear to be in a helicopter, high above the Eternal
City, enjoying as it were a God's-eye view. As the helicopter glides toward St. Peter's, in the slowest of slow
motions, above the Forum, along the Tiber, as the or-
chestra swells into a dawn chorus, a message flashes up at
the top of her screen:

*Doctors have announced that Emperor Hirohito's condition
at 8:30 this morning was as follows . . .*

Hiroko had already read the announcement about the
Emperor's health a hundred times that day, and every day
for several months. It was as integral a part of her tele-

vision screen as the morning clock. 10:03. We are now above the Castel Sant' Angelo, that enormous slab of Roman brickwork situated on the banks of the Tiber which guards the main approaches to the Vatican. Hiroko, who has never seen a castle quite so perfectly circular and perfectly formidable, makes a mental note to tell her husband, Teibi, that one day they really must spend an afternoon in this obviously old European city.

Temperature of body 100.9. Pulse 92. Blood pressure 148/ 170. Breath count sixteen per minute.

The update on the Emperor's health obliterates most of Michelangelo's dome. This seems to irritate not only Hiroko (and me) but also the camera, which abandons its slow glide into St. Peter's and suddenly nosedives into a confusing detour, emerging, somehow, in another part of Rome above the Colosseum. Hiroko is puzzled (so was I). The elegant melon-shaped dome that had been filling her screen clearly belonged to a more complicated age. This Colosseum was so remorselessly round and simple, so bossy, so ponderously European! Why had the camera taken this detour into Rome's ancient past? *"They call it the Eternal City,"* answers a female narrator, taking her cue from a wide shot of the Arch of Constantine. *"It has a history that stretches back forever. And a future that stretches forward, forever . . ."*

The prospect of this endless future excites the camera. Having zoomed in on one of the splendid spear carriers perched on the architrave of the Arch of Constantine it now zooms out and up, spins around, and emerges from its spin focused perfectly on a female bottom in a tight black miniskirt.

Emperor Hirohito has been discharging blood.

The bottom undulates down a catwalk, pauses, and poses before a crowd of enthusiastic photographers. We appear to be at some sort of clothes show. The Rome Fashion Fair? *"And so the Romans have created an extremely sophisticated high-fashion lifestyle. The old and the new coexist."* Hiroko disapproves of young girls wearing skintight midget-black minidresses that leave nothing to the imagination. Even her daughter, Yumi, has started wearing one this winter. The miniskirt is one European goody, Hiroko feels, Japan should resist. She's relieved when the camera escapes from the blush-making fashion fair as abruptly as it entered it, and resumes its slow-motion glide, at dawn, through the liquid gold sky, toward Michelangelo's dome. Leaving the Castel Sant' Angelo behind, it approaches St. Peter's head on along the Via della Conciliazione, laid out by Mussolini's Fascist town planners in 1936 as a suitably imposing introduction to the Vatican. Hiroko was taught at school that the European Romans always built their roads in unwavering straight lines, which marched like an army across Europe and Asia. She was not taught, because these things were never mentioned, that when the Italian Fascists drove the Via della Conciliazione through the jumble of medieval streets of the old Borgo straight into the heart of the Vatican they destroyed forever the effect intended by the architect Bernini of a welcoming piazza around St. Peter's. Bernini, in 1656, planned that his ring of columns should encircle the perimeter of the piazza and greet visitors to St. Peter's the Italian way, with a hug, like a pair of embracing arms.

To emphasize the welcoming nature of the new Catholic church, the NTV editors cut to an image of Papa John Paul II passing through a cheering Vatican crowd in his Pope-mobile, waving, on his way to his weekly Wednesday audience with his congregation. (Why are there so many nuns in the audience and so few priests? Hiroko wonders, reading my mind). Hiroko likes him. He has even been to Japan, the most traveled, the most televised pope in history. Later on in the program the narrator will inform Hiroko that John Paul II's first papal visit to Japan (no converts, millions of fans!) was one of the reasons why NTV came to be involved so directly in the restoration of the Sistine ceiling. But for now, having taken Mussolini's route up the center of the Via della Conciliazione into the middle of Bernini's piazza, the flying slow-motion camera makes an unexpected dink to the right, soars up over Bernini's colonnade, and finds itself in among the Vatican's roofs. And there it is, the Sistine Chapel, a curious castellated building, tall, box-like, with a dark arcade running along its upper story, a hiding place for Renaissance archers, explains the narrator. From the outside, the chapel is a fortress, not a church. Nothing about this austere exterior hints at what lies within.

"Inside this building is the most inspirational artwork that man has created. That Michelangelo created. As Goethe wrote . . . " Goethe? On NTV? Hiroko does a double take. So

do I. The world really is changing. *"As Goethe wrote: 'We cannot know what a human being can achieve until we have seen this fresco.' "*

Of course Hiroko recognizes the scene that now fills her screen. She has seen it hundreds of times before, stenciled on ashtrays, embroidered on the dishcloths you buy at Seibu Department Store, inlaid into beautiful Japanese marquetry boxes on sale at the airport, on T-shirts, on balloons. A bearded old man in pink robes reaches out his hand toward another man, younger, naked. The camera zooms in on their fingers. They stretch but do not quite touch. We are up in the international airspace of myths, where an inch can stand for an eternity.

"The powerful body of God, who is giving energy to Adam, who is our ancestor. Without whom we wouldn't be here. But five hundred years of turbulent history have damaged Michelangelo's great creation. It is cracked. Dirty. Covered in soot. Now, the biggest, the most important restoration project of this country has been mounted here in the Eternal City. A project the whole world is watching."

Emperor Hirohito's condition at 9:30 this morning was as follows: temperature of body 100.7

Fortunately, the Emperor's medical report appears in the sky above Adam and God and does not interfere significantly with Hiroko's view of her *gaijin* ancestor. What muscular shoulders he has! And what a small penis— before and after cleaning. *"The Nippon Television Network Corporation, together with the Vatican,"* explains the narrator, *"has been restoring the largest and greatest masterpiece of Western art since 1982."*

NTV is best known for its quiz shows and its excellent baseball coverage, a popular middlebrow all-Japanese TV channel, with, until now, no record at all of supporting the arts. For twenty years the channel had, however, been broadcasting a religious program called "The Light of the Heart," which catered to Japan's tiny Christian minority. When John Paul II became the first pope ever to visit Japan in 1981, he met Yosaij Kobayashi, chairman of the Nippon Television Network Corporation.

"I was privileged to be granted an audience with His Holiness, perhaps due to Nippon Television's endeavors toward world peace," explained Kobayashi, surely deluding himself. As Quentin Crisp once said: "Poland is not a country; it's a state of mind." One of the chief distinguishing features of this state of mind is the ability to remember the well-being of the pocket and the well-being of the soul at exactly the same moment. Pope John Paul II, the former Karol Wojtyla of Krakow, swiftly brought up the sponsorship of the Sistine Chapel, on which work had begun in 1980 and for which financial support had long been sought. "The pope," Kobayashi later confirmed, "graciously allowed us to participate in this project of the century."

The Vatican has never been slow to capitalize on its assets. The Sistine Chapel could not have been built without a very vigorous campaign of selling indulgences, fiscal corruption, and creative nepotism on the part of Julius

II's uncle, Sixtus IV. But even given this raunchy mone-
tary history, the fact remains that persuading a Japanese
TV company best known for its quiz shows and soap
operas to pay for the restoration of the Sistine ceiling
represented a fisco-ecumenical coup of some significance.
The restoration deal cost NTV three million dollars. In
return they received exclusive rights to all the photographic material of the cleaning and continued to do so
for three years after the work was completed. At the time
Hiroko Katayama was sitting in her Tokyo kitchen, eyes
glued to the NTV special on the Sistine ceiling, the
restoration campaign was already seven years old.

*Pulse 92. Blood pressure 148/170. Breath count fourteen.
No discharge of blood.*

*"And this is a diary of those seven years, a diary of the
restoration project that is transforming the Sistine Chapel. Michelangelo is coming back to life! But first an intermission. This
program is being brought to you by Kirin Beer. The Yamaha
Corporation. BMW Japan. Orient Finance. The Kawasaki
Steelyard. And Cupid Mayonnaise.*

10:15. Hiroko makes a mental note to buy some
more Cupid Mayonnaise. So do I.

The ceiling is not just the culmination of the Sistine Chapel. It is the constantly interrupted, much-worked-for, fiendishly delayed, triumphal climax to Rome itself. Getting to see it involves an unusual amount of effort even for the hardened museum-goer. The Vatican does its part by sending you on a twisting detour from St. Peter's piazza to the papal tradesman's entrance, out the back, along the terrifyingly impenetrable Vatican wall, right and then left up the Via Leone IV, constantly on guard for pickpockets. Street vendors start working on you long before you enter the Vatican museums. They taunt you with posters, postcards, and placards. Hands, hands, are everywhere. Most belong to Michelangelo's Adam and God. But a few are attached to gypsy women with gold teeth who clutch your arm and push their infant daughters under your feet. When you advise them to sell their gold teeth if money is all they need, they hiss dark Romany curses at your departing shadow. Their ancestors probably stood in the same place muttering the same curses at Michelangelo, a famously frugal man. Bombarded, most days, by the sun, this papal detour is a notoriously long half-mile that many do not complete. This is only the beginning.

A Vatican queue is not like other queues. Other queues grow shorter the more you wait. Vatican queues grow miraculously longer and louder as coachloads of sneaky Italian teenagers somehow insinuate themselves between you and the ticket office. Before you can say *"Scusi"* you are halfway back to the piazza again. Vatican queues are impressively multiracial, and the babble of many tongues soon grows into a biblical roar. The great wait to board Noah's ark must have been like this.

When Frank Lloyd Wright designed the Guggenheim Museum in New York he cleverly distributed the galleries around a spiral ramp that leads you upward in a kind of quiet artistic ascension. There is no doubt that Wright was influenced by the original great helicoidal ramp, the monstrously large example situated just down the road from the Vatican in the Castel Sant' Angelo. The Castel was begun by the emperor Hadrian in A.D. 135 as his own mausoleum. Inside it, Hadrian's twisting spiral still sucks you up into the building like a claret cork.

The Castel Sant' Angelo's giant helicoid ramp also influenced the architects of that extremely unlikely Fiat car factory at Lingotto in Turin. Lingotto, the ultimate Modernist folly, had two vertiginous spiral ramps at either end, one providing ingress, the other egress to a full-size testing track at the top of the building (which you may have seen Michael Caine racing around in *The Italian Job*). When those little Fiats of the twenties, dizzy from the spinning, finally emerged into the daylight at the top of the ultimate car factory, that too must have seemed like a glorious mechanical ascension.

But the spiral is a devious shape. Just as in the opening of a wine bottle you push your corkscrew down in order to pull the cork up, so a certain G. Moro, in 1932, while working for Pius XI, discovered how to build a spiral ramp that makes you feel as if you are descending deep into the Underworld as you climb up it. Moro cast his ramp in bronze, called it the Helicoidal Stair, and positioned it at the entrance to the Vatican museums. It still stands there, dark, wicked, daunting. Of course you get to the top in the end, but every step of the way visitors are made to feel as if G. Moro is forcing them to take the long route around. Unfortunately, this is the main public entrance to Michelangelo's masterpiece, so up the sinking spiral you must go, noting perhaps the papal arms embossed on the sides, for they contain the oak tree and crossed keys of Sixtus IV and his nephew Julius II, the chief papal protagonists of the Sistine Chapel. Eventually you emerge in the booking hall, having achieved a kind of dogged ascension of your own. This is only the beginning.

It was the secretary-general of the Vatican museums,

Walter Persegati, who in 1971 finally found a way to guide two million visitors a year through seven kilometers of galleries to inspect the two hundred thousand or so art objects divided up among the fourteen different museums in the Vatican collection. Persegati, according to his own recollections, was watching a hospital movie and was impressed by the way that the men carrying the emergency stretchers were guided to the operating room by a simple system of color-coded lines on the floor. He determined to do the same at the Vatican. The result is a fiendishly complicated one-way system involving various chunks of the spectrum that lead you a merry dance around the Vatican holdings. The dance lasts one and a half, three, three and a half, or five hours, depending on whether you are following purple, beige, green, or yellow. This kaleidoscopic labyrinth makes it entirely impossible to reach the Sistine Chapel quickly.

Even if you have a very fine mind capable of memorizing the route, and are prepared to skip over ropes and argue with the guards, the distances involved are simply too great. The guards, in any case, are unlike guards in any other museums. In other museums guards are old, kindly, often immigrant, pleasantly part-time. At the Vatican the guards are young and Italian. Their job is to prevent the kind of attack that the man with the hammer launched against Michelangelo's *Pietà* in St. Peter's in 1972. All the Vatican guards are trained in judo. "There are so many enemies of art," explained Signor Persegati to *The Times* of London in October, 1988. "But the real danger is from vandals. They damage works because it is

an effective way of carrying their message to the world."
From his medieval headquarters in the Vatican offices
Signor Persegati inspects the queues on a TV monitoring
screen. He tells *The Times* that his recurring nightmare is
that one day someone with undetectable plastic explosive
will find a way into the Sistine Chapel.

There is, I think, little danger of that. Signor Persegati's color coding will surely confuse the bombers just
as radically as it confuses the rest of us.

But it is certainly true that the Sistine ceiling is now
one of the new breed of vulnerable art masterpieces that
must spend the rest of its natural life being unnaturally
protected from the public—like the fractured *Pietà* kept
behind thick glass in the nave of St. Peter's, like Picasso's
Guernica stored behind a bulletproof screen in the Prado
in Madrid, like Leonardo da Vinci's twice-attacked cartoon
of the Virgin with St. Anne in London (which first had
ink showered over it and was then fired at with a shotgun),
like Velázquez's *Rokeby Venus,* slashed by a British suffra-
gette, like the Rembrandt in Berlin that had acid thrown
at it. The Sistine ceiling is a marked work of art. It has
entered the world's collective unconscious as something
special, privileged, famous. The same storms of psychotic
envy that drive maniacs to shoot popes, presidents, pop
stars, and painters drive them into attacking famous works
of art. With surreal consequences. *Guernica* has become a
giant goldfish in an unbreakable bowl. Michelangelo's
Pietà sits in a papal bank vault where once there was a
chapel. Intractably separated from its public by bazooka-
resistant glass, the poor masterwork can only sit there

looking ever more valuable. The Sistine ceiling, its cleaning over, will also spend the rest of its history as a heavily guarded fetish. But for the time being, all you have is a weird sign in the ticket hall saying: "The electronic devices are sensitive to the excessive proximity of persons."

We persons haven't even reached the chapel yet. There is still Signor Persegati's obstacle course to complete. Up and down the corridors we go, in and out of courtyards, out onto the shaky external drawbridges engineered to keep the one-way system going, down into the museum bowels and through the outrageously awful collections of modern religious art, two million of us a year, careering around the various papal additions, studiously following green, yellow, purple, or brown, striking out down some of the longest corridors ever built, past maps of the world as it was in 1580 (a good deal simpler to get around than it is today), up, down, in, out, and around we go, an army on the march, searching for Michelangelo.

Finally we emerge into a cramped burlap-lined staircase that acts as a chicane, slowing us down and thinning us into a single file for the final approach. If you have been following the green route, you approach from above. Yellow followers come up from below. A taped voice informs all of us in four languages that there is to be no flash photography in the Sistine Chapel, and we are requested not to talk. Presumably no one actually hears this somber request for silence. Because the noise coming from inside is deafening.

THE IMAGE

Andy Warhol had been dead a week when his name appeared on the bottom of a letter sent to Pope John Paul II on March 5, 1987. The letter concerned the paintings by Michelangelo in the Sistine Chapel. It had among its other signatories the illustrious Abstract Expressionist Robert Motherwell; the inventor of Combines, Robert Rauschenberg; James Rosenquist, the Pop artist; and the Bulgarian who had wrapped the Pont-Neuf in Paris and thrown a curtain across the Grand Canyon, the conceptual wrapper, Christo. They certainly formed a prestigious modern pantheon. But none of them had shown much interest in, or conspicuous knowledge of, Renaissance fresco before.

In particular it seemed strange, ridiculous even, that Warhol, the celebrated proponent of fifteen-minute fame, Walt Disney on Dope, as J. G. Ballard called him, should have felt it necessary to come to the rescue (as he saw it) of a painting that not only had been seriously famous for five hundred years but that also seemed to promise, in its iconography, that the wicked and the sinning would be damned for eternity. If Michelangelo's bearded white God up in the Sistine vault had felt the need to expel Eve from paradise for picking forbidden apples, what would the Almighty have made of the antics of Edie Sedgwick, Candy Darling, Sugar Plum Fairy, and the rest of Warhol's Factory supertarts? If tasting forbidden fruit was sinful, what about learning how to inject yourself in the buttocks without removing your Levi's, Brigid Berlin–style? And yet Andy Warhol owed something important to Michelangelo Buonarroti. He owed him his place in society.

The letter sent to Pope John Paul II by Warhol's ghost and the pantheon of American artists was a protest against the cleaning of the Sistine ceiling. It was polite in an arrogant way: "We fully recognize the noble purpose of those who have authorized the restoration . . . and the extensive research that was undertaken in preparation for the task. We respectfully propose a pause in the restoration, however, to allow a thorough analysis of the results obtained so far. This precautionary measure would provide an opportunity to review all of the options available for the continued preservation of the master work." The casual assumption by our celebrated signatories that the restorers of the Vatican's most prestigious possession—the most famous work of art in the Western world—were proceeding in their task without "a thorough analysis of the results obtained so far" says much for the ignorance of modern artists about the methods of modern restorers. In fact, as we shall see, the Sistine restoration was being undertaken with the aid of ultimate state-of-the-art computers, buzzing, flashing, growling in their hi-tech kennel up on the scaffolding. Every morsel of information was being gobbled up and classified.

It later transpired that Andy Warhol had agreed to becoming a signatory of the Sistine letter just before he died and that he had been an enthusiastic if secret Catholic for most of his adult life. Indeed, Warhol and Michelangelo had more in common than we might have expected. Both were deeply, even darkly, religious men. Both were good with words, Michelangelo in his sonnets, Warhol with his dictations into a cassette recorder that eventually emerged as cute wisdoms and *Diaries*. Both liked to mix in high society and can honestly be described as snobs. Both tried to cover up their true origins as if ashamed of them. Both were interested in—no, obsessed with—money. Both developed intriguing confessional relationships with glamorous female confidantes, Michelangelo with the pious poet Vittoria Colonna, Warhol with Bianca Jagger. Both were extremely influential artists whose influence on others, alas, was not always healthy. Andy was the most famous artist of his era and the "divine" Michelangelo Buonarroti was certainly the most famous of his. Both were homosexual in a repressed, asexual way, and their homosexuality had a crucial bearing on their work.

But all these are circumstantial and merely personal similarities. What really makes Warhol and Michelangelo comparable figures is the way that, in both their cases, during both their lives, it soon became impossible to separate the myth of The Artist from the humble flesh and blood of the human being.

Michelangelo was the original tortured artistic spirit, and he could thus claim to be the first ancestor of all modern artists. Ariosto's "Michael, more than human, Angel divine" became, and remains, an iconic likeness of God-driven Genius Incarnate: broken nose, shaggy biblical beard, terrifying *terribilità*. To much the same degree, Warhol turned into an icon of himself: white wig, black clothes, blank face. Whereas Michelangelo liked to pretend that he was of noble birth, Andy liked to pretend that he came from nowhere.

Late in his life Warhol succeeded in doing something Michelangelo never accomplished. In 1985 he produced a portrait of Michelangelo's greatest patron, the awe-inspiring pope and instigator of the Sistine ceiling project, Julius II. He did it by copying Raphael's *Sistine Madonna,* in which Julius appears on the left kneeling before the Virgin in his full papal attire. Where Raphael gave Julius the attributes of St. Sixtus, an obvious allusion to his uncle, Warhol gives him the attributes of a special offer in a New York delicatessen. Il Terribile has $6.99 written above his head, a papal bargain if ever there was one. It later transpired that Warhol was working on a whole series of Renaissance images before his death, copying Botticelli, Leonardo, Raphael.

Andy Warhol: *"Publicity is like eating peanuts. Once you start you can't stop."*

On January 4, 1557, the kindly prior of the Innocenti in Florence picked up his quill and pondered the significance of a good deed he had just performed: "How much difference there is between one man and another! Three German gentlemen had a great wish just to *see* Michelangelo, and I introduced them; he received them very kindly to their great satisfaction." Eighty-year-old Michelangelo had become one of the unmissable sights of Rome, like the Colosseum or the Arch of Septimus Severus. He had become what the Japanese today describe as a living treasure. He was more famous than any artist had ever been before and had acquired what we can confidently call a cult following.

The cult had a high priest, Giorgio Vasari, Michelangelo's biographer and all-round Boswell. It had its own improved likeness of Michelangelo, which it placed on his tomb when he died. Byron, in 1818, visited the sacred tomb in midcanto in *Childe Harold:*

"In Santa Croce's holy precincts lie/ Ashes which make it holier . . ."

The Michelangelo cult had its own idea of what the master's teachings meant and its own favorite Michelangelo anecdotes, which it treasured as profound wisdoms and which have come down to us in numbers. While Andy Warhol said that he would like to be reincarnated as a big ring on Elizabeth Taylor's finger, Michelangelo is said to have said that a man paints with his brain and not with his hands. He was the first artist whose paraphernalia were collected, his utterances, his correspondence, his bills, and his memories. Around 480 of his letters survive; there are eight hundred more sent by others to him. Then there are petitions, contracts, statements, and assorted legal documents that bear his name. He appears in other people's memoirs and is the chief protagonist in two examples of tricky Renaissance "faction," convoluted dialogues in which the writer carries on an imaginary conversation with Michelangelo and speculates upon what Michelangelo might have said had he actually been there. He wrote poems, of course, and 327 survive, the finest literature ever produced by an artist (compare them with Picasso's plays, which can probably claim to be the worst literature ever produced by an artist). Scholars have spent five hundred years picking through this Michelangelesque mountain of paper, and until the Japanese-sponsored cleaning of the Sistine Chapel proved them wrong, they believed they knew more about Michelangelo than they did about any other artist of the premodern era.

Shakespeare was born in the year in which Michelangelo died, 1564. Yet we know next to nothing about him, not even enough to silence once and for all the crackpot critics who periodically emerge from dark literary lagoons claiming that Shakespeare did not exist. Michelangelo, on the other hand, actually had three biographers—Giovio, Vasari, Condivi—working on his existence while he was still alive, supplying it with the finest motives, shaping it, improving it, until they had created a Michelangelo we can still recognize easily enough today:

Michael, more than human, Angel divine, as played by Charlton Heston, as scripted by Irving Stone. The Life of Michelangelo was a fancy creation in its own right. Gutenberg's printing press, invented about 1450, made it possible for Michelagnolo di Lodovico Buonarroti Simoni, a bureaucrat's son from Caprese in Tuscany, baptized on March 6, 1475, to remodel his own image, and become the first artistic hero of the paper age.

The belief that Michelangelo's talent was godlike, more than human, is the chief distinguishing feature of the Michelangelo myth. Benvenuto Cellini was a goldsmith, a convicted sodomist, and an outrageous rascal, who left behind the funniest art memoirs of the Renaissance. But this entertaining braggart is never funny about "the divine Michelangelo Buonarroti, prince of sculptors and painters." Michelangelo literature is thick with such habitual ascriptions of divinity. "He has proceeded from conquest to conquest," trumpets his enthusiastic biographer Vasari, "never finding a difficulty which he cannot overcome by the force of his *divine* genius." Crucial to the maintenance of this image was the establishment of a lie: that Michelangelo, the genius, was self-taught.

Ascanio Condivi was Michelangelo's assistant, a trusting man, who, judging only by his written *Life of Michelangelo,* was exactly the sort of naive, unthreatening lackey that insecure great men always like to have around them. Condivi's *Life,* published in 1553, goes out of its way to present Michelangelo as a perennial victim, of misunderstanding clients, of plots by jealous rivals (notably Bramante and Raphael), of ill winds, ill health, and an ignorant public. Art historians agree—for a change—that Condivi's *Life* should be seen as a kind of ghosted autobiography. And also that it was a reply to Giorgio Vasari's version of Michelangelo's life, which had been published three years earlier. Vasari, a sycophant as well but a questioning one, had claimed that Michelangelo studied painting as a young man in the workshop of Ghirlandaio, the solid Florentine fresco painter responsible for two of the scenes on the lower level of the Sistine Chapel. Condivi—who must have been told otherwise by Michelangelo himself—claims that this was not true: Michelangelo did not study painting under Ghirlandaio. Because he was entirely self-taught.

But no. In 1568 Vasari, the questioning sycophant, brought out yet another, revised edition of Michelangelo's life and in it, in a splendid display of Renaissance self-importance, he huffily provided documentary proof, signed by Michelangelo's father, that young Buonarroti had indeed been apprenticed to Ghirlandaio in the years in question. And of course he must have been. No pope of authority, as Julius II unarguably was, would have given over a site of ten thousand square feet situated above the altar of the most prestigious chapel in Christendom to a man who had not even been trained to paint. Was Michelangelo practicing duplicity or had he merely started believing in his own legend?

One thing is certain. For the best part of five hundred years we have conspired to believe the legend with him. It was easy. We too want our divinely inspired geniuses to pop up miraculously from nowhere. Just before he died Michelangelo burned a stack of drawings. "He often abandoned his work," explains Vasari, "rather he destroyed many of them, as I know that a little before he died, he burned a great number of drawings, sketches and cartoons made by his hand, in order *to appear nothing if not perfect*" (my italics).

When the cast list for *The Agony and the Ecstasy* was announced, a journalist asked Charlton Heston: "Don't you think you're too tall to play Michelangelo?"

"No. I'm too small," replied Heston.

Cecil B. deMille prepared for the making of *The Ten Commandments* by traveling to Rome, to the church of St. Peter in Chains, to look at Michelangelo's *Moses.* He was lucky enough to live in an age when Rome was still made up of real buildings and was not yet the bundle of mysterious plastic parcels undergoing restoration that the city has since become. Whenever I visit St. Peter in Chains it is under scaffolding. DeMille was fortunate. The tomb of Julius II was surrounded by a solid church and, sitting in the middle of the tomb, eyes flashing, was the celebrated statue of Moses. DeMille was impressed. And is quoted as snapping: "If it's good enough for Michelangelo, it's good enough for me." He decided there and then that his Moses must look like this and set about finding an actor to play the biblical giant. He quickly settled on Charlton Heston, having first—in a remarkable display of in-depth research—drawn a white beard onto a photograph of Heston and pronounced the likeness "amazing." Heston in his own memoirs remembered it thus:

"Somebody brought to DeMille's attention the startling resemblance between my face and that of Michelangelo's Moses in the church of St. Peter in Chains in Rome. It's true. The resemblance is unmistakable. The nose is broken in the same place. The cheek bones are the same. . . ."

The nose is broken in the same place? The cheekbones are the same? Clearly Heston, who broke his own nose playing football and who once made a living posing as a male model, was confusing the features of Moses with those of Michelangelo himself. Two Michelangelos, a real one and an imaginary one, can be pleasantly compared and contrasted at the Capitoline museums housed in a fine example of the master's own architecture perched on the top of the most precious of Rome's seven hills. One of these Michelangelos is painted, a scruffy brunet by Jacopino del Conte. The other is carved out of glamorous black marble by that traditional worshiper of great men, A. N. Onymous. The painted Michelangelo is a small brown man. He has sallow skin that seems a couple of sizes too large for him. It droops about his face like the skin on an old olive. His beard is straggly and needs trimming. He is one of those compact Mediterranean men who cannot grow thick body hair. He has Modigliani shoulders, a broken nose, sunken cheeks, beady eyes, and the unassuming air of a Renaissance greengrocer. It is possible to imagine this man haggling over the price of goats in the market but difficult to envisage him mastering the Sistine ceiling. He is like Picasso in the flesh, like Miró in the flesh, like the real Andy Warhol—smaller than you imagined.

The other Michelangelo, made of marble, has the shoulders of a boxer. He has been wrapped in great swathes of imperial cloaking, placed on a gorgeous polychromatic pedestal and flanked by two bronze Roman *Geese,* which are, in fact, ducks. They pleasantly undermine the air of noble sadness that is the marble Michelangelo's main attribute. Where the painted Michelangelo looks you nervously in the eye, the marble one studies the ground at your feet in an impressive display of troubled self-absorption.

A. N. Onymous derived this official cult image from the likeness by Michelangelo's disciple, Daniele da Volterra, that sits on the great man's tomb in Florence. This mythical Michelangelo still has the broken nose, high cheekbones, small eyes. But his skin fits. His beard has substance. And those solid middleweight's shoulders look as if they could bench-press the *Farnese Hercules.* There is something else. A biblical air, something saintly. Stone plays perceptual tricks on its audience. When Michelangelo's face was carved out of black marble, his dark and straggly beard was transformed into a growth that appeared white and thick and biblical. New beard in place, this marble Michelangelo could now pass for Noah, Moses, Jeremiah, Joseph, Nicodemus, St. Bartholomew, a veritable arkload of biblical wisemen. The stone Michelangelo had metamorphosed from a brunet with a straggly beard into an Old Testament prophet.

I would go further and claim that the collective unconscious is always severely tempted to make a connection between the biblically bearded Michelangelo and the traditional Catholic image of God the Father, especially Michelangelo's own God the Father, as portrayed on the Sistine ceiling. Freud wrote almost nothing about art. In this, as in so much else, he set his disciples a good example, which they, alas, did not follow. But one of the two essays on the subject Freud did produce finds him sitting in St. Peter in Chains in exactly the same spot as Cecil B. deMille, looking up at Michelangelo's *Moses*. Freud's prose swiftly grows B-movie purple. "Sometimes I have crept cautiously out of the half-gloom of the interior . . . ," he whimpers, unable to look the great paternal statue in the eye. When Freud did find the courage to stay and gaze up, he too was mightily impressed: "The giant frame with its tremendous physical power becomes a concrete expression of the highest mental achievement that is possible in a man, that of struggling against an inward passion for the sake of a cause to which he has devoted himself." That is not Moses. That is a description of the mythical Michelangelo who carved *Moses*.

Freud's only other substantial essay on art concerns the genius of Leonardo da Vinci. Leonardo also looked like some bearded white-haired Old Testament prophet, and it seems reasonable to assume that Freud's own subconscious had spotted that this was how we wanted our geniuses to look, like superfathers, like the Renaissance's invented image of the Almighty.

Charlton Heston not only played Moses in *The Ten Commandments*; he also doubled as God, or at least as God's voice: a slowed-down tape recording of Heston's own voice was turned, electronically, into the sound of the Almighty. But it was not until 1965 that Heston was able to complete his own cinematic Holy Trinity when, confusingly, his startling resemblance to Moses won him the role of Michelangelo in *The Agony and the Ecstasy.* "I've played so many men of whom statues have been made," he later bragged. "All agony and no ecstasy," quipped an unkind critic. And it's true that no man ever suffered for his art quite so profusely as the celluloid Buonarroti.

In a quandary about what he should paint on the Sistine ceiling, he goes off into the Tuscan wilderness, climbs a hill, and looks up at the sky. The clouds begin to vibrate. They billow and coalesce. Slowly they form themselves into a familiar scene. A hand is stretching out. A famous finger. God is creating Adam. . . .

According to Hollywood, Michelangelo did not invent the Sistine ceiling. He copied it.

Inspired by Charlton Heston, I too have Michelangelo hallucinations. There I am sitting in St. Peter in Chains, in the same row as Cecil B. deMille, Freud, Charlton Heston, Giorgio Vasari, and Yvonne De Carlo, who played Moses' wife in *The Ten Commandments.* I'm looking over at the marble Moses and in my hands I have a copy of Vasari's life of Michelangelo, from which I read aloud: "No other modern work will bear comparison (nor indeed do the statues of the ancient world). Michelangelo expressed in the marble the divinity that God first infused in Moses' most holy form."

Three Germans who had come to Rome just to *see* Michelangelo and who expect silence in their churches turn around and shush.

Sorry. Er, *Verzeihung.* I continue reading Vasari to myself:

"And well may Jews continue to go there (as they do every Sabbath, both men and women, like flocks of starlings) to visit and adore the statue, since they will be adoring something that is divine rather than human."

Oh no. That D-word again. Something snaps. Springing up to look Moses in the eye, I knock over my chair. "Nonsense, Vasari," I cry, startling a huddle of Japanese tourists gathered around Moses, persuaded to come and photograph Rome by a gorgeous NTV film they had recently seen on the cleaning of the Sistine ceiling.

"Nonsense. Don't you see that by underestimating Michelangelo's humanity and exaggerating his divinity you are lessening his actual achievement? Michelangelo invented this on his own."

A large group of Israeli pilgrims who had filed in a moment earlier on some sort of mildly illicit Saturday excursion—after all, the Second Commandment expressly forbids the worship of graven images—look round for an attendant, a priest, a Gentile, anyone.

"On his own! On his own!"

I career blindly out of the church. Just before the door I barge into a bearded American in a Hawaiian shirt and knock something out of his hand. "Sorry," I mutter. "Sorry." I pick it up and shove it back at him. It's a photograph of Gene Hackman onto which the guy in the shirt seems to have drawn a beard.

THE CEILING

As I stood within kissing distance of Michelangelo's Adam, so close that I felt the need to stoop in order not to rub my head on the Sistine ceiling, I had a flash of insight concerning Michelangelo's vision of Eve. This high up, in this company, in this place, any dumb thought is apt to seem deeply significant. But squinting over the restorer's scaffolding away from Adam's creation toward the scene of his upcoming seduction and expulsion from Paradise, I could see Eve very clearly—more clearly than all but a handful of humans had seen her since she was painted in 1510. And quite definitely she had the body of a man.

Eve's weight-lifter's thighs and pectorals, her pythonesque biceps, the curious way her waist was a man's waist rebuilt four inches higher than usual, gave her body a masculine outline that the two awkward appendages attached like rubber balls to her front did nothing to feminize. Only her hands and feet were convincingly girlish. Either Michelangelo had never seen a naked woman in his life, or he had and considered the information gained irrelevant.

> *In the room the women come and go*
> *Talking of Michelangelo*

To witness from touching distance the restoration of the greatest work of art in the Western world, you first had to negotiate a small obstacle course of Vatican bureaucracy. Among the forms you had to sign, the most important was the one declaring that in the event of an accident up on the scaffolding you would not hold the Vatican responsible for the damages. In the event of an accident up on the scaffolding, there would not have been much left of you to seek damages with. It was an awfully long way from the realm of Michelangelo to the clever geometric chapel pavement below, which of course you never saw, for it was packed solid, all morning, with a rich assortment of mortals.

In the corner of the Sistine Chapel was a covered tower, with guards outside it. Inside the tower, if the guards let you pass, was a ladder that looked as if it was made of matchsticks and a tiny yellow cage elevator powered by what appeared to be rubber bands and a lawnmower motor that phutt, phutt, phutted you sixty feet up into the air. Going up in that rickety elevator for the first time was one of the most exciting experiences of my life. Above me divided as cleanly as the flavors in a Neapolitan ice cream were two completely different Michelangelos, one monochrome, one colored; one pessimistic, the other optimistic; one old and one new. The Sistine restoration was many things, but at its height and most obviously of all, it was a magnificent piece of theater in which we the audience could stand below and make a classic choice:

"The day exists where the sun leaps and plays, / Distributing its full and generous light," wrote Michelangelo in Sonnet XLII. "Oh night, Oh sweetest time although obscure, / All things you consummate with your own peace," he U-turned in Sonnet XLIV. As judgments go, this choice between the dark old Michelangelo and the bright new one was outrageously Solomonic.

On the way up in that rickety elevator, you had to slide past a bloody murder: the beheading of a screaming Egyptian who had maltreated a Jew, Botticelli's beginning to the story of Moses, painted on the lower walls of the chapel. Then a large bulging knee appeared, and above it a heavily bearded head, deep in thought, Michelangelo's Jeremiah, a self-portrait and the inspiration for Rodin's *Thinker*. A few phutts more and you were up there in the gods.

The restorers worked on a scaffolding designed in imitation of Michelangelo's own, for even in scaffolding design he was an overachiever. What surprised me immediately about this compact platform was not how clever it was but how communal. There was an arkload of people up there trying to squash against Michelangelo. There were keen American professors who would later accuse the Vatican restorers of ruining the Sistine masterpiece and assorted fee-paying foreign students from Rome's restoration school (who were not so keen). There were Japanese filmmakers who looked too young to have seen *The Agony and the Ecstasy* and Italian glitterati who looked rich enough *not* to have invested in it. (What were they doing up there; had the sacred scaffolding become a stop on their social rounds?) There were Belgians, Poles, and a Korean, people with limps, and on my second visit, a woman who grasped my wrist in the elevator and told me that she suffered from terrible vertigo. (What was she doing up there; had the sacred scaffolding become, like Lourdes, a place of healing pilgrimage?) And then there were the three wise Vatican restorers who had created an aerial kingdom for themselves, a kind of caravan home in the clouds, with comfy chairs, computers, telephones, a visitors' book, a marvelous roof, of course, and a wizard's assortment of bottles and brushes to dab and scrub with. They received their daily visitors with impressive politeness and a strong sense of promotional responsibility. For these were the 1980s, and being a restorer was no longer the obscure backroom occupation it had once been. Being a restorer had become a glamorous addition to the performing arts. Besides, there was plenty of room for all of us. The cleaning of the Sistine ceiling was to destroy many myths about the travails of Michelangelo, but the first one I began to doubt when I stepped out onto this busy subway stop in the sky was the myth of the desperate isolation of Michelangelo's creative vigil.

I was also surprised, and pleased, by the seeming irreverence displayed by the most senior of the three restorers, Signor Gianluigi Colalucci, who, in explaining to me the various complexities of both the cleaning process and the original painting, never missed the opportunity to give Michelangelo's fresco a good firm slap and rub, like a groom enjoying his special relationship with a favorite horse. No one would ever again be on such terms of pleasing familiarity with the fresco. Once this cleaning was completed, the Sistine ceiling would revert to its original role: as a massive art-historical presence that was largely mythical.

For the time being, however, there it was, within touching distance and quite irresistible. Positioning myself beneath the celebrated gap between God's finger and Adam's, I reached up and added a third digit to the configuration. I cannot tell you what a thrill this silly musketeer's gesture gave me.

In the room impeccably turned-out Italian schoolkids
in unending herds come and go
Talking (loudly) of anything but Michelangelo.

From close up, Michelangelo's untreated masterpiece looked surprisingly rough. The plaster was crisscrossed with wide cracks. Some had been brusquely filled with stucco during earlier Sistine restorations; others had had bronze brackets driven into them to stop sizable chunks of masonry from plunging into the babbling crowd below and killing some Italian teenagers. Jeremiah, who was ahead of me on this particular visit, might have approved of such an accident, for he loathed the sinners of Judah and was the most doomy of all the prophets, Christian and pagan, that Michelangelo assembled on the Sistine ceiling. But Jeremiah's cleaning was still to come, and his likeness to Michelangelo himself was still largely obscured by a murky growth of salts. Salts had been plaguing this ceiling in patches from the first wet winter Michelangelo began work here, in 1508.

The Sistine Chapel is a formidable building, "a cliff of brick" from the outside. The walls of its basement story are ten feet thick. But ever since it was built the chapel has had a rather troubled structural history. In 1522 a lintel above the entrance door split, killing the Swiss guard who was accompanying Adrian VI into the chamber at the time. During the conclave of October, 1525, the world's cardinals had to be pursuaded to enter the chapel, so convinced were they of its imminent collapse. The roof is the most vulnerable Sistine expanse of all and has always been a problem. If the vault had not been a problem, and had not cracked in the spring of 1504, causing one of the Vatican's masters of ceremonies to complain that it had "split down the middle," it would still probably be decorated today with a star-spangled sky painted after 1481 by a certain Permatteo d'Amelia.

Water leaking through the plaster, causing patches of discoloration and the accumulation of various deposits of sulphates and calcium carbonates, would trouble the fresco throughout its history. Early in 1509, according to Condivi, Michelangelo found that the work he had completed in the upper reaches of the vault was being attacked by mold. He had in fact been painting Genesis back to front, having begun not where God began, by making Light and Dark out of Chaos (which the Almighty does at the other end of this ceiling with impressive sangfroid), but with the Drunkenness of Noah, where man showed God how capably he had learned to degrade himself. To the superstitious and supersensitive Michelangelo, that first outbreak of mold in the winter of 1508–1509 must have seemed like a major God-sent disaster. He consulted the architect, his friend and fellow Florentine Giuliano da Sangallo, about the salt deposits, and Sangallo's advice helped him to cure the infestation—temporarily.

These same salts will surely find a way to continue discoloring the ceiling in perpetuity, whatever the three wise restorers achieved in the 1980s. Salts always find a way. That is why the explosion of gunpowder in the far-off Castel Sant' Angelo in 1797 did so much damage. The salts had undermined the fabric of the fresco. Not only did one of the decorative *ignudi* recoiling from Noah's Drunkenness tumble down into the realm of the mortals but so did the tree beneath which some of the damned were sheltering on the right-hand side of the Flood. The missing chunk was never replaced. It is still up there now, filled in with clever 1980s computer-designed toning, so that you hardly notice it.

I am grateful to the NTV film crew for flying over the Sistine Chapel in a helicopter at the beginning of their Michelangelo spectacular, thereby allowing us to study the roof from above. It is obvious enough where all the water must collect and where the salts will do their worst. It is Jeremiah's misfortune to be situated beneath a particularly wet roofing black spot, at the intersection between the Sistine's vault and its walls, or—in Michelangelo's painted scheme of things—between Heaven and Earth. This uncertain terrain is occupied all the way around the Sistine perimeter by a mighty ring of seers, seven Christian prophets and five pagan sibyls, all gazing into the future of humankind, and all looking notably troubled. For nearly five hundred years, Jeremiah, one of Michelangelo's most heavily bearded self-portraits, had been singled out for special attention by the Sistine salts. I have to admit that he looked, on this particular visit, like a man with a future as a stalactite.

> *In the room three giggling Malaysian nuns looking*
>   *slightly out of place in their stern Catholic habits*
>   *come and go*
> *Talking of Michelangelo*

Stepping out of the elevator and into the weird celestial divide between darkness and light (imagine one half of the sky at midday, the other at midnight) I had found the three wise restorers working on the Creation of Adam: "And the Lord God formed man of the slime of the earth, and breathed into his face the breath of life; and man became a living soul . . . "

Seen from close up, the most celebrated components of this component-packed ceiling, the nearly touching fingers of God and Adam, were quite evidently the handiwork of someone other than Michelangelo. A wide crack divided the Maker from the First Man, and it was not "The Homer of Art" himself who effected the running repairs and repainted Adam's fingertips at the end of the sixteenth century. It was probably the admiring cleaner, Giovanni Carnevali, some of whose infills of wax and resin were being kept by the restorers of the 1980s, others removed.

Carnevali's fingertips were darker than the rest of Adam's flesh. So they have played a curiously significant part in the mythology of the Sistine ceiling, emphasizing the divide between man and God just that fraction more than Michelangelo intended. The 1988 restorers gouged out Carnevali's infill and gave Adam a brand new pair of fingertips with which to reach out across the abyss of creation. (What complicated frustration there must be to being a restorer, keeping to yourself the amazing secret: I painted the most famous fingers in the world!) Months later, I viewed this new hand of Adam from below. Was it my imagination or had the great touch-that-never-was lost a fraction of its impact?

The new additions were being done with downward strokes, in watercolor, so that future generations could easily recognize them and dispense with them should they wish to. And wish to, at some point, they surely will. For every generation, like God creating Adam, reinvents the Sistine restoration process in its own image. What we had here was not the ultimate cleansing that Hiroko

Katayama, back in Tokyo, was promised in the Michelangelo special on NTV. It was a display of superrestoration, 1980s style.

If you shone a torch across Michelangelo's handiwork, as these restorers liked to do, for they were natural Italian crowd-pleasers transparently aware of the drama they were involved in, a strange thing happened to the Sistine ceiling. Shadows appeared, and gulleys. You could see that the surface of the vault, so flat-looking and cinematic from the ground, actually undulated like a lively stretch of the Umbrian hills. Far away into the distance it rolled, once round the clip-on cleavage of Eve down to the nudity of the drunken Noah, each day's work leaving its lunar bumps. The restorers were pleased, for they were able to chart Michelangelo's progress across the quarter-acre of painted ceiling with absolute precision. I was pleased because there was so much self-evident humanity in the Divine Michelangelo's bumpy vaultscape.

Fresco is the most macho of the great painting methods. It is a method that, like Michelangelo himself, has been much mythologized, notably by fanatical Florentines like Vasari: "Fresco being truly the most manly, most certain, most resolute and durable of all the other methods, and as time goes on it continually acquires infinitely more beauty and harmony than do the others. Exposed to the air fresco throws off all impurities, water does not penetrate it, and resists anything that would injure it." The Sistine ceiling proves Vasari to have been wrong about the medium's invulnerability—as we have seen, fresco's weakness is salts. But Vasari was right about its magic.

To stand within touching distance of this madly undulating vault is to become aware of just how gorgeous a gorgeous slab of fresco can be.

The basics of the medium are easy enough to understand (and studiously explained to Hiroko Katayama with samples and graphs by NTV in their Michelangelo special): an area of wet plaster is laid down on a specially prepared ground, and the artist applies colors to it. These colors fuse with the wet surface as it dries, leaving a union of plaster and color that is indelible. Each fresh area of plaster to be painted is called a *giornata,* a day's work.

The disadvantages of fresco are obvious: every area of wet plaster has to be finished in one go before the plaster dries. The medium puts enormous pressure on the artist's first touch. Not only are you working against the clock but if you make a mistake you must do what Michelangelo did to one of Christ's ancestors in the Achim and Eliud lunette: take a hammer to the ancestor's head and start again. Fresco is not a medium for nervous painters. Nervous painters should stick to oil paints. "Oil painting," Michelangelo is reported to have muttered, "is fit only for women and lazy people like Fra Sebastiano." Fra Sebastiano was Sebastiano del Piombo, a friend for thirty years before they fell out and Michelangelo turned (characteristically) nasty on him.

The advantages of fresco have to be seen from close up to be understood, and fully believed. Take God's beard. From below it looks like nothing much, a biblical beard, after all, is a beard is a beard, is it not? No, it is not. A beard, when painted by Michelangelo, in fresco, is a whirlwind of long first touches. There are so few of them that every one can still be easily followed as it corkscrews into perfect hairiness. This is the sort of economy you expect from Matisse, or Picasso. "Paint direct and don't maul your paint," said the English intimist Walter Sickert to his pupils four hundred years later. Michelangelo's wristy Sistine shorthand is as futuristic as the Renaissance could be. Modernism was alive and well in 1510, sneakily disguised as the fresco technique.

The famous reclining Adam took only four *giornate.* The God who made him took three. And, as Signor Colalucci explained further, standing beside me patting Adam on the rump, it is important to remember that a man could work on more than one *giornata* in a day. Michelangelo probably darted around this scaffolding from scene to scene with some alacrity.

In *The Agony and the Ecstasy* it was the length of time the Sistine ceiling took to paint that was impressive. Up there in the flesh, with God's wavy beard flapping above my face, it was the speed at which Michelangelo worked that amazed me. The same thoroughly audacious hand that took no time at all to paint God created the white of Adam's eye by the simple expedient of leaving an area of plaster unpainted. Adam's famous little penis consisted of just two brushstrokes that must have taken all of two seconds to apply.

Is fresco the greatest medium of expression that has ever been available to an artist? Signor Colalucci seemed to think so. His eyes misted over and he quoted Cennino

Cennini's fifteenth-century maxim that fresco is "the sweetest and most attractive way of working there is."

In the room German tourists with bazooka-sized cameras
   (no flash) come and go
Snapping at Michelangelo

The last parts of the Sistine fresco to be completed by Michelangelo were the lunettes painted quickly in the illusionistic niches just above the windows. Here he gathered together the ancestors of Christ as listed at the beginning of Matthew's gospel. If the Sistine vault represented Heaven and the great ring of prophets below it represented a kind of spiritual bridge between Heaven and Earth, the lunettes, squashed beneath the feet of the twelve bulky seers and sibyls, were obviously meant to represent our mortal world: cramped, busy, agitated, and, for the best part of five hundred years, absolutely filthy. They were the dirtiest of all the frescoes, more or less uncleaned since they were completed, at the very end of the Sistine campaign, 1511–1512. The last frescoes to be painted, the lunettes were the first parts to be cleaned. Work on them started in 1980, a year before the pope's fateful visit to Japan. Their cleaning produced shocking results. No one, no scholars, no restorers, no American Modernist admirers of Michelangelo, expected them to be so full of outrageous color. Art historians who had grown up on the dark myth of the Sistine ceiling had been doubly convinced of the darkness of the Sistine lunettes.

Scientists had a theory. They claimed that the lunettes were so dirty because the walls of the Sistine Chapel were colder than the roof and some five hundred years of soot, dirt, and candle-gunk from braziers and torches found it easier to accumulate there.

Scholars also had a theory. They claimed that Michelangelo deliberately painted the lunettes darker than the ceiling for various complicated symbolic reasons. "The sphere of shadow and death" is how the grandest of the great twentieth-century Michelangelo scholars, Charles de Tolnay, described the world of the lunettes, contrasting it with "the sphere of light and eternity above it."

What actually seems to have happened is that for five hundred years nobody thought the lunettes worthy of much maintenance. They grew darker and darker because the various cleaners who attacked the ceiling during the Vatican's intermittent restoration campaigns inevitably ignored them. The divine sphere of light and eternity at the top of the vault was what interested the Vatican. Not the emphatically earthly sphere of hunchbacks, sleeping old men, yapping children, and all the other lively inhabitants of the Sistine lunettes. Because the lunettes had been allowed to grow dirtier and dirtier, they were the section of the Sistine ceiling that provided the most dramatic surprises when cleaned, and viewed up close.

The Michelangelo who began emerging from beneath five centuries of papal gunk was a painter in a furious hurry. So much so that he was found to have produced one of the lunettes—a family portrait of Roboam and his pregnant wife that is ten feet tall and twenty feet wide— in a single session, in one huge *giornata*. It is as large a *giornata* as has ever been found. Michelangelo worked on Roboam so quickly that he left hog's hairs from his brush embedded in the slumped ancestor's leg. The restorers found them and treasured them. The painting of the lunettes provides impressive proof of Michelangelo's fast hands. The cleaning of the lunettes indicated that Michelangelo was just like the rest of us: he dawdled, dawdled, dawdled, and then rushed around madly finishing the job. By the time he reached the last lunette he was in such a hurry that he had to dispense with most of Aminadab's family and only painted a husband and his wife. The result is a striking single-figure simplicity, which the restorers enhanced considerably when they revealed that the dress worn by Aminadab's spouse as she combs her golden hair was not the mousy brown number that the world expected but a dress of gorgeous, dramatic pink. It was these unexpected colors that most offended the small group of American scholars who began mounting a vociferous opposition to the cleaning as soon as the Sistine lunettes were unveiled.

> *In the room visiting art historians taking advantage of*
> *a once-in-a-lifetime opportunity come and go*
> *Talking of Michelangelo and asking whether or not the*
> *restoration has irrevocably ruined the fresco.*

We know him as Boaz, but Michelangelo calls him "Booz." Booz was an old farmer from Bethlehem. According to Ruth, whose story takes up the eighth book of the Old Testament, Booz was a good man. Ruth is sent to pick corn in Booz's field and Booz, seeing the young widow at work, engineers preferential treatment for her so that she can take away the maximum amount of corn with the minimum amount of effort. "May the Lord bless Booz," says Ruth's mother-in-law, Naomi, a sentiment Michelangelo presumably disagreed with, for he has immortalized Booz in the Sistine Chapel as an old idiot.

Ruth, unlike Michelangelo, appreciates the kindness of Booz. She goes to him while he is asleep, and lies at his feet. Booz awakes, admires her, and agrees to look after her. They marry. Even though Ruth is a Moabite and Booz is a worthy of the tribe of Israel, this mixed marriage is one of the few such marriages in the Bible that work. They have a child, Obed, who becomes the father of Jesse, who was the father of David, whose son was Solomon, who sired Roboam, and so on in splendid onomatopoeic ancestral leaps until we reach Christ himself.

The occupants of the Sistine lunettes are a most animated collection of biblical types, stretching, snoring, leaning, lamenting, muttering, making faces, the men talking to themselves, the women hung with children like radiators hung with washing. In these vivid portraits Christ's genealogy is given a unique human form as one large eccentric Holy Family. Booz plays the ugly step-grandfather.

Michelangelo's outrageous caricature of him shows an old man with a can-opener nose, a gravity-defying beard that juts skyward, and a Fool's stick, which he holds in front of him and shouts at. The Fool's stick has— as all Fool's sticks are meant to have—the Fool's own likeness carved in its handle. The likeness has opened its mouth and is giving as good as it gets. Booz shouts at his stick and the stick shouts right back. Booz is definitely the ugliest, and the most evidently mocked, of all the ancestors. I stare and stare at him, wondering why. Nothing the Bible records specifically about Booz explains Michelangelo's character assassination.

It is one of the more important discoveries to be made up on the scaffold of the Sistine Chapel that Michelangelo enjoyed his work and had an impish sense of humor. You see it obviously enough in some of the caricatures of Christ's ancestors. But it is also evident in minor details and the witty use of paint. God may have taken an entire Genesis day to create the Earth, but Michelangelo only took a couple of moments: a few quick flicks of green and he had covered the planet in vegetation. You can see the quick touch and the wicked sense of humor complementing each other perfectly in the fidgeting bronze devils squeezed into the tightest corners of the ceiling, the narrow triangular niches wedged between the lunettes and prophets. These bronze devils grimacing madly are the Sistine Chapel's version of cathedral gargoyles, Gothic stowaways in the High Renaissance.

The devils are a firm reminder of the fact that Michelangelo's first recorded work was not a copy of some perfectly poised Greek marble athlete but a reworking of the wild, monster-filled engraving of the Temptation of St. Anthony by the minor Northern Renaissance master Martin Schongauer. Schongauer filled his temptation scene with Bosch-like nasties, pecking and sucking away at poor

St. Anthony. According to Condivi, the young Michelangelo admired Schongauer's engraving so fiercely that he took himself off to a fishmonger's to study the color and slitheriness of fins and gills. This Gothic side of Michelangelo is given its head in the lunettes: in the dozing hunchback Amon, in the wild-eyed Joseph above the entrance, and, above all, in the madly chattering portrait of Booz on Booz's Fool stick. Never was the knob of a stick so keen on cursing.

Victor Hugo also tells Booz's story in a pleasing poem, "Booz Endormi" (Booz Asleep). "This old man owned fields of . . . barley. . . . His beard was silver like an April stream." Hugo's Booz, old, wifeless, dreams an impossible dream in which love appears and puts an end to his loneliness. Waking from his sleep, he finds Ruth at his side, young, loving, and compliant. "Women looked at Booz more than at a young man, / For the young man is fair, but the old man is great," wrote Hugo, suffering a serious attack of wishful thinking.

None of which explains why Booz should be branded a fool by Michelangelo. Is the old man being ridiculed for marrying a younger woman—reasonably likely, given Michelangelo's own sexual proclivities? Or is Michelangelo mocking Booz because he has been taken advantage of by an uninvited foreign woman who came and stayed? Either way, that well-worn proverb, there's no fool like an old fool, seems to be being illustrated. In the same way, the sleeping hunchback in the Amon lunette seems not to be heeding the sound advice delivered in the Book of Proverbs that when a lazy man sleeps "poverty will attack him like an armed robber." Christ's ancestors occupy the lower, human levels of the Sistine Chapel. And Michelangelo has given them human faults aplenty.

Not so Ruth. Ruth is one of those melancholy Madonnas glowing with goodness in whom Michelangelo also specialized. Since she has been cleaned, the beautiful Ruth blushes as pink as a rose. She is a paragon of maternal beauty. Painting paragons of maternal beauty is just about all that Michelangelo ever did with woman. When asked why he had made his Madonna in St. Peter's so baby-faced, Michelangelo replied: "Do you not know that chaste women retain their fresh looks much longer than those who are not chaste? How much more, therefore, a Virgin." That is not the remark of a genius. It is the remark of a sexual ignoramus who believes in old wives' tales (and the Bible's proverbs).

There is another reason to stare and stare at the Booz lunette. The cleaning has revealed that sometime after it was finished, a papal improver, in an attack of prurience, painted out the breast that Ruth was offering to the baby Obed. This breast was rediscovered in the cleaning. It now hangs, like all Michelangelo's breasts, completely unconvincingly, from Ruth's chest, a fleshy smudge poking out of the breathtakingly gorgeous camellia pink of Ruth's robe, a robe that used to be muddy brown. Booz too has had a complete change of clothes since his cleaning. He once wore olive. He now wears something bright yellow, an outré little tunic set off with purple tights. O, Michelangelo, how you have mocked Booz when you could have shared in his happiness! "I am a widower, I am alone, and evening falls upon me, and I bend, O my God!" wrote Victor Hugo, begrudging the old man nothing. O Michelangelo, why have you given Ruth the udders of a cow?

> *In the room sour-faced Polish clerics from the papal*
> *inner circle come and go with their heads bent into*
> *their breviaries.*
> *Not looking at Michelangelo.*

In *The Agony and the Ecstasy,* Charlton Heston costars with Rex Harrison, who plays the domineering Pope Julius II, who commissions the ceiling and spends most of the movie pacing up and down like an expectant father shouting, "When will you make an end to it?"

"When I am finished," replies Heston, between clenched teeth, for he plays a kind of Michelangelo sandwich squeezed between the scaffolding and the Sistine roof.

This cinematic re-creation of the great fresco takes place on the summit of a bizarre mountain of planks and timbers that is supposed to represent Michelangelo's scaffolding. The mountain grows not only upward but sideways too, down the length of the chapel, from window to window until it fills the room, a kind of timber Mt. Sinai from which the Mosaic Michelangelo descends quickly when he is fainting (by sliding deliriously down a rope) and very slowly when he is called upon to conduct a defense of his work before a college of angry Vatican cardinals. The argument takes place on the steps near the bottom of the scaffold. Looking up at the first Sistine

nudes, the angriest of the cardinals turns to Rex Harrison/
Julius II and shouts: "He has turned Your Holiness's own
chapel into a Greek temple."

"I'll tell you what stands between us and the Greeks,"
interjects the wild-eyed Heston/Michelangelo. "Two thousand years of human suffering."

According to Condivi, it was the papal architect of
St. Peter's, Bramante, who tried first to invent a scaffolding on which Michelangelo could successfully work. Bramante seems to have envisaged some sort of hanging
structure suspended above the chapel, for which holes had
to be drilled in the roof. Michelangelo protested and
devised a scaffold of his own, the first crucial appearance
in his work of what we might call an engineering or
architectural bent. Forty years later, he was to climb his
own engineering Everest when he designed the enormous
dome of St. Peter's, but for the time being, his problem
was how to construct a scaffolding that would be strong
enough to support a team of workmen but that would not
block off all the light and that, most important, would
allow the papal ceremonies to continue in the chapel
below.

What the Vatican restorers at the start of the 1980s
cleaning campaign duly discovered was a series of oblong
holes pushed into the walls of the chapel just above the
cornice and the windows. Into these openings Michelangelo inserted wooden struts, which jutted into the chapel
and provided the supports for an arched bridge that could
now be built across the great internal divide. This scaffolding, supported on the cornice high above the floor,

had obvious advantages over the cinematic mountain of wood. It was lightweight and actually grew more secure the more pressure was applied to it. It did not block off as much light. And it certainly allowed the chapel to be used for services while Michelangelo worked above. It was an exceedingly clever invention, which the 1980s restorers reconstructed exactly in lightweight metal.

As this restoration progressed, the illusion of Michelangelo, the thunderous God-driven genius, was gradually replaced by the reality of Michelangelo, the possessor of an astute, practical, human intelligence. From the moment of its erection the Sistine scaffolding played a vital part in this transformation, in the removal of the "Nietzschean mists."

But Michelangelo's original scaffold was not popular with everyone. The miserable Master of Papal Ceremonies, Paris de Grassis, who kept a diary but who never once mentions Michelangelo by name, records on June 10, 1508, that Vespers of the Vigil of Pentecost were being disrupted. "In the upper portions of the Chapel the scaffolding was being constructed, causing a lot of dust, and the carpenters did not stop as I ordered. The Cardinals complained of this. Moreover, when I reproved the carpenters several times and they did not stop, I went to the Pope who was angry with me, as though I had not admonished them. The work continued without permission even though the Pope sent in succession two of his chamberlains, who ordered the work stopped, which was finally done with difficulty."

De Grassis supplies contemporary proof that the scaffolding was constructed above the heads of the worshiping clergy. And that builders in the Renaissance were just as deaf as they are today.

Michelangelo lived through the reigns of thirteen popes and worked for seven of them, an extraordinary success story of relentless papal patronage. He was, as we know, a small man. Charlton Heston was not. So Rex Harrison, who was a sturdy six-footer himself, wore built-up shoes in an attempt to look Heston in the eye during the interminable painter-to-pontiff confrontations out of which the bulk of *The Agony and the Ecstasy* was made. "As the film went on," Harrison remembered, "it seemed to me that he was growing. Eyeball to eyeball he was once more a couple of inches taller than I. He must have grown through sheer tenacity."

Groucho Marx, on hearing how much the film had cost, said to Charlton Heston: "You could have saved a lot of money if you'd painted the Sistine Chapel floor instead of the ceiling."

Those scenes in which Charlton Heston was seen flat on his back feverishly dabbing at his fresco, and miraculously completing it, were shot using a very tricky special effect developed specifically for the movie. What he was actually doing was *uncovering* a huge photographic recreation of the painting, which technicians had hidden beneath a thin layer of gunge. The set, which won the art director an Oscar nomination, was at the time the biggest indoor movie set ever created, a full-scale reproduction of the Sistine Chapel built in Dino de Laurentiis's Rome studio. In 1965 it cost nine million dollars. That was three times more than NTV contributed to the entire Sistine restoration of the 1980s.

In fact, the Japanese support proved visibly preferable to most other typical 1980s art sponsorship deals, particularly those involving pushy Italian companies. Where the Italian approach to sponsorship in the 1980s seemed to demand that the sponsor's name and achievements be given greater prominence than the work of art, NTV's was a model of sensitive discretion. So much so that when conversation up on the scaffolding turned to them, no one up there could understand why the Japanese had been so reluctant to exploit their exclusive rights to their material. Quietly, shyly almost, the NTV photographers and camera crews floated about Michelangelo's revolutionary scaffold putting together the most thorough visual record of a major art restoration that is ever likely to be assembled. And they hardly said a word while they were doing it. Everyone else involved in the project more than made up for them.

In the room, a tape programmed to go off automatically when the noise inside the Sistine Chapel reaches a certain decibel level begins the laborious task of asking for quiet in a long assortment of the world's leading languages. Everyone stops talking of Michelangelo and starts complaining about the noise made by the infernal blabbermeter.

THE HARDSHIP

Charlton Heston is flat on his back lying on a plank sixty feet up in the air, dabbing away at a Hollywood replica of the Sistine ceiling. The sweat running in rivulets from his brow finally finds the route of maximum annoyance it has been searching for and pours into his eye. Heston wipes the sweat off with his sleeve. The sleeve is dirty with paint, so that too gets rubbed into his eye. Then a drop of fresh color from the ceiling drops into his eye as well. Everything up there is eagerly responding to the laws of Newtonian physics and making a beeline for Charlton Heston's eyes. As he falls off the scaffold, temporarily blinded, and begins the long, tumbling descent to the floor that is Heston's stuntman's finest moment in *The Agony and the Ecstasy,* a line of Edward Dahlberg's comes to mind. "Suffering," wrote Dahlberg, in *Because I Was Flesh,* "is too precious to be shared."

The idea that Michelangelo painted the Sistine ceiling on his own while lying flat on his back for four years is one of the most tenacious of all the great Michelangelo fantasies. Its origins can be traced back to a mistranslation of Michelangelo's first biography, thirty-one lines written in Latin by Paolo Giovio, Bishop of Nocera, sometime between 1523 and 1527. Giovio describes Michelangelo's posture while painting the Sistine ceiling as *resupinus.* This was assumed to mean "on his back" by the various Michelangelo commentators who spent five centuries enthusiastically emphasizing his agony at the expense of his ecstasy. A more accurate translation of *resupinus* would be "bent backward."

Since Bishop Giovio's account there have been numerous elaborations on the great Sistine Discomfort Story. Others have suggested that Michelangelo painted lying on his side, on his knees, propped up on one elbow, or suspended from the roof in a specially developed hanging chair. In the mind's eye of his admirers, Michelangelo has been put through an entire *Kama Sutra* of difficult positions from which to complete his masterpiece. Some of the most macabre of these projections of discomfort have been squeezed out of the subconscious of the solemn translators of the amusing sonnet Michelangelo sent to his friend Giovanni da Pistoia, in which Michelangelo himself cheekily exaggerated the agonies of painting the Sistine ceiling. This amusing sonnet is one of the most heavily translated poems in European literature. It is also one of the consistently worst translated poems in European literature. The normally elegant Elizabeth Jennings began her rendition thus:

> *Like cats from Lombardy and other places*
> *Stagnant and stale, I've grown a goitre here;*
> *Under my chin my belly will appear,*
> *Each the other's rightful stance displaces.*

It certainly sounds as if Michelangelo is in some pain, but who can have any idea what he is doing? The questions are numerous. What does a stagnant and stale cat from Lombardy look like? If a goiter is a swollen neck, why should cats from Lombardy, or indeed from other places, be particularly prone to it? And what, pray, is the rightful stance of a chin? We must know the answers if these truly dreadful lines are to inspire any image at all of Michelangelo at work. Creighton Gilbert, in his translation, the most popular among Michelangelo scholars, goes into greater detail on the puzzling Lombard cat analogy:

> *I've got myself a goiter from this strain,*
> *As water gives the cats in Lombardy*
> *Or maybe it is in some other country;*
> *My belly's pushed by force beneath my chin.*

It seems that cats in Lombardy, or maybe in some other country, get goiters from the water. What light does this shed on Michelangelo's discomfort? Peter Porter, the Australian poet, opens up his notably surreal contribution by pooh-poohing the water theory:

This comes. of dangling from the ceiling—
I'm goitered like a Lombard cat
(or wherever else their throats grow fat)—
it's my belly that's beyond concealing
it hangs beneath my chin like peeling.

Peter Porter is thus the first to place Michelangelo under the vault of the Sistine Chapel. Both Elizabeth Jennings and Creighton Gilbert are guilty of concealing this vital information that Michelangelo's belly is feeling like peeling, reeling on the ceiling. At least all three bamboozled wordsmiths are agreed that Michelangelo's terrifying ordeal has only just begun. Before Michelangelo, artists worked for their art. After Michelangelo, they suffered for it mightily.

It cannot be a coincidence that the four most celebrated artists to be given the dubious honor of a major biopic were all proven and notorious human sufferers, balancing their creative lives on a knife-edge of pain. Who can forget Kirk Douglas sobbing and ranting his way to greatness as Van Gogh in *Lust for Life*?

GAUGUIN/ANTHONY QUINN: *Why don't you shut up! If you have to slobber don't do it over me.*
VAN GOGH/KIRK DOUGLAS: *Aaaachchch!*

Or poor old crippled Toulouse-Lautrec hobbling between the absinthe bottle and the brothel in John Huston's *Moulin Rouge.* (This is the same Toulouse-Lautrec whom the girls in the cathouse called "the Teapot" because his small body had such a large spout attached!) Most recently, in Derek Jarman's *Caravaggio,* the suffering artist sweats, murders, and buggers his way to an early death, a driven homosexual with a thing about knives. Unlike these other fantastic celluloid creatures, the mythological Michelangelo survived to a ripe old age, being nearly ninety when he died. But this longevity, far from being a cause for celebration, is presented in the myth as a curse. The longer Michelangelo lived, the more he suffered. Nowhere more so than back up on the Sistine scaffold, where Creighton Gilbert is still busily listening to the howls of agony:

> *My beard toward Heaven, I feel the back of my brain*
> *Upon my neck, I grow the breast of a Harpy;*
> *My brush, above my face continually,*
> *Makes it a splendid floor by dripping down.*
>
> *My loins have penetrated to my paunch,*
> *My rump's a crupper, as a counterweight,*
> *And pointless the unseeing steps I go.*

In the ugly annals of Michelangelo translation, there is no more blatant disregard of the grace and grammar of English than that spectacularly awful line: "And pointless the unseeing steps I go." Michelangelo, it seems, has dozed off on the Sistine scaffolding and started sleepwalking. At this point Peter Porter gets completely carried away:

> *My beard points skyward, I seem a bat*
> *upon its back, I've breasts and a splat!*
> *On my face the paint's congealing.*

Loins concertina'd in my gut,
I drip an arse as counterweight
and move without the help of eyes.
Like a skinned martyr I abut
on air, and, wrinkled, show my fate.
Bow-like, I strain towards the skies.

According to the information supplied so far, the blind, batlike Michelangelo is balanced on one buttock high above the pavement of the Sistine Chapel impersonating a bow-shaped Lombard cat with a fat neck. No wonder painting this ceiling was held to be a trial. "God will not look you over for medals, degrees, or diplomas, but for scars," wrote the epigrammatist Elbert Hubbard, taking the Michelangelo line on life.

The man who started all this with his innocent use of the word *resupinus,* Paolo Giovio, may have been the Bishop of Nocera, but his theology was clearly in need of tightening. "Among the most important figures," he observed, looking up at the Sistine ceiling in his tiny biography of Michelangelo, "is one of an old man, in the middle of the ceiling, who is represented flying through the air." If the Bishop of Nocera cannot recognize God, what hope is there for the rest of us? But Giovio recognized a legend that needed knocking down to size when he saw one, and near the end of his thirty-one–line biography he attempts a little character assassination of his own. Michelangelo's nature, he remembers, "was so rough and uncouth that his domestic habits were incredibly squalid."

Just as our age has its florid Michelangelo myths, so did his own times. As far as the popular imagination of the Renaissance was concerned, Michelangelo was famous for living in squalor. Even the sycophantic Vasari records visiting the old artist late in his life and finding him wearing dog-skin booties, which had been on his feet for so long that he could not take them off without also removing a layer of skin. This sense of the squalor and suffering that surrounded Michelangelo is now five hundred years old. And it is the backcloth against which the great hardship myth grew up. Back at the poem, Michelangelo's agonies are piling up.

Broadly speaking, the NTV commentator in Tokyo, who is also attempting a Japanese translation of the dreaded sonnet, takes the Creighton Gilbert line on the geography of the Sistine Chapel. The floor is below Michelangelo, and not, as others are suggesting, above him.

> *From the brush the paint is dripping*
> *And my face has spotted patterns like the floor*
> *And my body is bent like a bow.*

If only some of this admirable Japanese clarity had rubbed off on Peter Porter.

> *No wonder then I size*
> *things crookedly; I'm on all fours.*
> *Bent blowpipes send their darts off-course.*

This image of Michelangelo painting the Sistine ceiling on all fours, presumably by holding the brush in his teeth and jumping up, like a dog from Lombardy, or some other place, is one of the most vivid mutations of the great hardship myth. Jennings doesn't mention the blow-pipe. The NTV commentator has the bent weapon down as "a musket." Gilbert is less specific:

> *Borne in the mind, peculiar and untrue*
> *You cannot shoot well when the gun's askew.*

Too true. The point has come at which Elizabeth Jennings's Michelangelo surveys the extraordinary physical tangle he finds himself in and comes up with a marvelous understatement. This is, he concludes: *"A hard position whence my art may grow."*

The truth is that Michelangelo was the most enthusiastic of sufferers. He was clearly one of those Conradian mortals who could not be truly happy unless they were suffering. That same billowing imagination that he brought to his art he also brought to the construction of his own misery. His letters back to his family in Florence at the time when he was working in Rome on the Sistine fresco are filled with paragraph after paragraph of vivid emotional blackmail, in which his holy suffering is contrasted with their devilish idleness. "For twelve years now I have gone about all over Italy, leading a miserable life," he wrote unpleasantly to his younger brother in June, 1509. "I have borne every kind of humiliation, suffered every kind of hardship, worn myself to the bone with every kind of labour, risked my very life in a thousand dangers, solely to help my family." The twelve years he was referring to were years of unparalleled critical and financial success that had turned a minor magistrate's son from Florence into a rich, landowning papal favorite, negotiating, at that very moment, to do what all Florentines do when they come into money—to buy a house in the country.

In a breathtakingly coy display of false modesty, Michelangelo spends the last three lines of his badly translated sonnet apologizing to his friend da Pistoia for the poverty of his achievement.

> *John, come to the rescue*
> *Of my dead painting now, and of my honor;*
> *I'm not in a good place, and I'm no painter.*

Or, if you prefer, the Australian finale:

> *Defend my labour's cause,*
> *good Giovanni, from all strictures:*
> *I live in hell and paint its pictures.*

Few until now have dared to suggest that Michelangelo painted the Sistine ceiling by walking around on a spacious scaffolding and reaching up with his brush. But that must have been how it actually happened. The reconstruction of his Sistine scaffolding has proved that the ingenious Michelangelo created a painting platform for himself that was roomy and convenient. There is also a delightful sketch of himself at work that he drew next to the amusing sonnet in his letter to his friend Giovanni da Pistoia. It shows quite clearly a painter standing on his feet reaching up with his brush to paint a ceiling. That drawing has always been there. But most commentators preferred to believe the evidence of their imaginations rather than the evidence of their eyes.

THE ENCOUNTERS

In 1543 a storm careering through the China Sea blew a Portuguese vessel bound north for Macao eastward instead, to a small island called Tanegashima off the southern tip of a landmass known as Kyushu. The Portuguese wanderers were well received by the locals, who saw the storm that brought these impressively large foreigners to their shores as a divine wind, or, in their own language, a *kamikaze*. The islanders were particularly excited by the firearms that the Portuguese adventurers carried with them. These were christened *tanegashima teppo*—"iron rods." It was not long before the locals began to manufacture the miraculous iron rods themselves. The Japanese economic miracle had begun.

In 1549 another Portuguese vessel arrived off the coast of Kyushu. It had on board a young Jesuit, Francis Xavier, a Christian zealot whose tireless missionary activity in the East was to earn him a snappy ecclesiastical sobriquet: the Apostle of the Indies. Xavier had with him two fellow Jesuits, two servants and three Japanese who had been won over to the faith in the south Asian stations and who were to act as translators. For it was Francis Xavier's ambition not only to convert all of these small, dark islanders to the True Church but also to make Japan the foundation stone of a massive new Christian empire in the East.

Xavier had previously preached in southern India. The experience had convinced him that the poor fisherfolk of Goa could never provide the basis for such an empire. The Malays and the Hindus were, he complained to his superior, too effeminate and visionary.

But the Japanese were something different. They already had a highly developed civilization and were handily organized into tight feudal compartments. It was Jesuit policy to concentrate their missionary energies on the feudal lords in the safe knowledge that the vassals would have no choice but to follow. Xavier himself came from a noble family in Navarre, and his letters home testify to the fact that he felt considerably more comfortable among the Japanese than he had among the humble fishermen of Goa. He was genuinely excited by the prospect of Japan's Christian future. "It seems to me," he wrote again to his superior, "we shall never find among heathens another race to equal the Japanese." He stayed until 1551 and left behind a Christian community of around a thousand converts.

When John Paul II took off from the Philippines on February 23, 1981, he left behind sweltering heat and Imelda Marcos, who had shadowed his every step, hoping, no doubt, that some of the traveling pontiff's thrilling popularity would rub off on her husband's hated dictatorship. The papal visit to the Philippines had been an obvious success. Huge crowds had greeted every appearance. But the Philippines were expected to welcome the pope with Bernini-like arms. The question that the commentators aboard the papal jet were asking, in the copy they were sending back to their editors, was: What lay in store? What would the uncertain pagan mix of Buddhists and Shintoists in Japan make of the Catholic Papa?

What no one was prepared for was the bitingly cold weather. An Arctic wind, or, in the language of the locals, a *kamikaze,* whistling down from Siberia, had packed the country in ice. Japan was experiencing the most severe cold spell in sixteen years. When the papal jet touched down in Tokyo, it was sleeting and raining and blowing up a storm. When the pope climbed down from his plane to place his customary peck on the tarmac, he felt the coldest foreign soil he had ever kissed. There were only a hundred or so people cheering his arrival. The Arctic blizzard had even driven the camera crews away. Later that evening, one TV channel in Tokyo carried news of the pope's coming. That was all.

For months before the visit, a battalion of Japanese admen had been beavering away unsuccessfully trying to raise the papal profile. The pope, it seems, had a serious image problem. Few Japanese had heard of him. Fewer still cared that he was on his way. The Catholic Bishops' Conference was forced to hire the country's two largest advertising agencies, Dentsu and Hakuhodo, to drum up some enthusiasm. Dentsu were told to stir up a *pope-boomu,* like the *panda-boomu* that had greeted the appearance in Japan of the first Chinese pandas. Or the *Mona-Lisa-boomu,* which resulted in huge queues of patient worshipers waiting for hours to stand for a second in front of Leonardo da Vinci's tiny masterpiece. How the French had been persuaded to allow the fragile *Mona Lisa* to embark upon a lengthy tour of Japan is a fisco-ecumenical mystery to rank alongside the Japanese involvement in the restoration of the Sistine ceiling. It is enough to notice here that artworks, like pandas, have become an invaluable currency in the exchanges of goodwill between nations. And that everybody wants a Nissan factory in their suburbs.

Back in the tour headquarters for the first papal visit to Japan, three-quarters of a million dollars were being plowed into the open-air mass that John Paul II was due to celebrate in a sports stadium in Nagasaki. Attempts were being made to disguise the mass as some kind of Christian pop festival. The pope was to be joined on the podium by the popular singer Agnes Chan (a Roman Catholic) and a rock band. A bright copywriter eventually dreamed up the slogan that was to be blasted out at the Japanese nation in the hope of jump-starting it into papal eagerness: "Young and Pope," said the slogan.

Dentsu also organized an exhibition of Vatican treasures, which toured Japanese department stores and which

had the gorgeous diamond tiara of Pius XI as its center-
piece. Low on artworks, high on carats, it was a show
that glittered like a jewelry counter. The admen worked
hard to promote a Christian image that could possibly
have some meaning in pagan Japan: the image of a modern, jet-setting, immensely wealthy church. But the image failed to engender much enthusiasm. When the papal
motorcade slid out of Narita airport into the Arctic winter,
only a few desultory protestors lined the route. One of
them held up a banner that swirled madly in the *kamikaze.*
"The Pope is a Beast," it said.

Julius II, as played by Rex Harrison, makes his entry
into *The Agony and the Ecstasy* on horseback, in full armor,
having just subjugated yet another of the enemy armies
that lie flattened about all corners of his reign like corn
after a storm. "He was," intones our grave Hollywood
narrator, "a better warrior than a pope." Rex Harrison's
biographer recalls that when Harrison was offered the
chance to play Julius, he bellowed with pleasure: "Now
there's a part! A Renaissance bull of a man, an unpopelike
pope, fighting duels, siring illegitimate children."

Giuliano della Rovere was born in Liguria on December 5, 1443, the son of a poor fisherman who happened
to be the only brother of Sixtus IV. Sixtus was the first
of the great papal nepotists. Of the thirty-four cardinals
he created in his pontificate, six were either his nephews
or his illegitimate sons. When he died the Roman mob
was so incensed by this familial favoritism that it ran-
sacked his apartments in the Riario Palace. Sixtus left

behind three great monuments to his reign. One was the Sistine Chapel, which he officially consecrated on August 15, 1483. The second was the Spanish Inquisition, which he allowed Ferdinand of Spain to implement in 1480. And the third was his nephew, Giuliano, the future Julius II, whom Sixtus had made a cardinal in 1471.

Giuliano della Rovere had deep-set eyes, compressed lips, and a pronounced nose. He was irascible and talkative. He always carried a stick, with which he is said to have struck irritating subordinates, including, in *The Agony and the Ecstasy,* Michelangelo. That he really was a willful and spiky man is borne out by all the contemporary accounts. According to the Venetian ambassador: "No one has any influence over him, and he consults few or none. Anything that he has been thinking about during the night has to be carried out immediately." Sometime in his youth Giuliano had contracted syphilis and sired three daughters. He was also renowned as a drinker (Greek and Corsican wine) and called an alcoholic by his enemies. According again to the Venetian ambassador, his dinner table was lavish, offering "caviar, prawns and sucking pig." Tortured by gout, Giuliano astonished everyone by his ability to ignore pain and get things done.

The conclave that elected him pope in 1503 was preceded by an energetic round of ecclesiastical bribery. Giuliano did not earn the papacy; he bought it. When the thirty-seven voting cardinals entered the Sistine Chapel, the result of their deliberations was already known. They duly emerged a few hours later, after the shortest conclave in papal history, with Giuliano della Rovere's name on their lips.

An observer from Ferrara, Francesco Guidiccioni, writing home the day after the announcement, opined: "People here expect the reign of Julius II to be glorious, peaceful, genial and freehanded. The Roman people, usually so addicted to plunder, are behaving so quietly that everyone is astonished." A pope who could inspire the Romans *not* to plunder—that truly was something out of the ordinary. Having been elected simoniacally, Giuliano surprised his own bribe-takers by proceeding to ban the practice of simony. Having been the recipient of spectacular nepotistic favors from his uncle, he himself became notably antinepotistic and spent nothing on his own nephews. Here clearly was an unusual man.

The thousand converts left behind by Francis Xavier in 1551 multiplied rapidly. By 1571 there were estimated to be thirty thousand Christians in Japan.

And these were not any old converts to the True Church. The Jesuit priests writing back to their superior paint a picture of spectacular enthusiasm for the new faith. In Funai, wrote Father Baldassar Gago, the new Christians came to catechism from two or three leagues afield. Those that lived farther out would arrive the day before and stay the night in the hospital. When they received the sacrament, their eyes flooded with grateful tears, which made the missionaries blush. A boy of eleven was asked how far his love of Jesus ought to extend. He replied: "As long as I am a Christian, even though I were to be cut into small pieces."

The new Christians also displayed an unprecedented fondness for the knickknacks of the new faith. When a statue of the Holy Lamb blessed by the pope arrived in port, it had to be broken into 1,530 pieces in order to satisfy all the claimants. Every day boatloads of men and women arrived at the Jesuit dockside asking to share in these Catholic goodies, begging for copies of the Sundarium or an Agnus Dei. Some of them, wrote Lodovico Froes, "pass eight days in prayer in order to merit the happiness of possessing such things." Here, then, was a *pope-boomu* of an intensity that the missionaries of the Society of Jesus had never before encountered in their travels.

By 1600 there were estimated to be seven hundred thousand Japanese converts to the religion of the cross. There seemed no reason in the universe to doubt that the dream of a Christian East, centered on Japan, would be a reality.

John Paul II spoke almost as many languages as he had souvenir hats from his travels. Back at the Vatican museum one afternoon, I follow an old Polish nun who is acting as a guide to a group of her country's pilgrims. She zooms them past the *Laocoon,* past the *Apollo Belvedere,* past the famous *Belvedere Torso,* past a museumload of classical art treasures, until she reaches a large marble bath that was once Roman but had since been used as a font for Christian baptism. She informs them how much this solid piece of marble weighs. They touch it and stroke it with awe. And she tells them a story of the pope's first day in office:

"He walked out onto the balcony over St. Peter's and looked out across hundreds of thousands of expectant faces. He began speaking to them in Italian, because of course our pope speaks eight languages. He was, he admitted, the first non-Italian pope for four hundred years. But what they had to remember—what they must never forget—is that the very first pope of all, St. Peter, was also a foreigner. How they cheered him on that day."

John Paul II's first appointment in Tokyo was a visit to the aging Emperor Hirohito, a descendant of the sun-goddess and the former divine ruler of Japan. The new pope and the ex-god met at the Imperial Palace.

Being a man from the north, John Paul II was not unduly worried by the Arctic weather conditions that threatened to preserve his visit in ice-cubes. As he hurried across the courtyard of the Imperial Palace in the drizzle, he refused an umbrella and strode ahead in his usual all-white canonicals and floppy burnt-orange hat. It was, the pope said, the first time he had stepped foot inside a royal palace. Hirohito walked unaided down the long flight of steps that led into his reception hall and continued out onto the palace porch, where he met his guest. They were soon deep in animated conversation in a curious mixture of three languages—English, French, and Japanese, the last of which the pope had been busily studying to add to his collection. Outside the perimeter of the palace, right-wing protestors with megaphones shouted slogans in shaky English. "Pope out!" they screamed.

The Japanese media were having difficulty finding a name for the Polish pontiff. How, after all, do you translate the title "Pope John Paul II" into Japanese? They settled on *Ho-o-Paulo-nisei,* which translates as "King of religion second-generation Paul." Followed by a polite *banzai.*

King of religion second-generation Paul's next major appointment was at Hiroshima, where he made a speech on February 25. "To remember Hiroshima," he said, "is to commit oneself to peace."

Rex Harrison looked good in armor, but rather silly in papal regalia. Much the same could be said, and was said, of the real Julius II. Julius led his first military expedition out of Rome on the morning of August 26, 1506. He left before sunrise, to avoid the midday heat, at the head of a column of nine cardinals and five hundred fully armed knights and their retainers. His short-term ambition was to conquer Bologna, which had proclaimed itself independent of papal authority. His long-term ambition was to restore the Holy See to its former glory and to recapture all the papal lands that had been lost over the years to various predatory neighbors. By the time he reached Orvieto, where he was due to meet the Florentine envoy, Machiavelli, the ecclesiastical vanguard of Julius's Bologna army had swollen to seventeen cardinals. "Only members of the Sacred College that were incapacitated by age or sickness were permitted to remain behind." Every morning he attended mass. Every morning his army was on the move before sunrise.

Six months later, a full-size replica of the Arch of Constantine was erected in front of St. Peter's to greet the papal army on its triumphant return. Bologna had submitted. Il Terribile had arrived.

"Everything had to bow to his iron will, even his own poor gout-tormented body," a body that he lugged around the battlefields of Italy at the head of a Vatican force that fought, sneaked, and bluffed its way to victory until almost all of the papal lands that had been lost by his predecessors were restored. He waged war against Venice. He waged war against the French and the Spanish. Having inherited a Christian banana republic that was flat broke and squeezed from all sides by greedy neighbors, he left his successor a powerful, rich, ambitious Roman Catholic empire. In strictly material terms, della Rovere, "hated by many and feared by all," was the most successful pontiff of the Renaissance. And when Rex Harrison turns to Charlton Heston and says, "You make a better priest than I do, Michelangelo," it is in the secure knowledge that he, Julius, makes a far, far better Renaissance pope than Michelangelo ever could.

Not everyone saw it this way, least of all the anonymous author of a hilarious dialogue purporting to eavesdrop on Il Terribile's attempts to talk his way into heaven, which appeared in pamphlet form on the streets of London at the time of Julius's death. To early-sixteenth-century Londoners Julius seemed far too venal a pontiff to be allowed through the Pearly Gates without a major argument. We first come across the fictional Julius, loitering outside heaven, trying to get into the door the key that he had been given as a successor to St. Peter. It does not fit. Julius fiddles with the lock like a drunk who has stumbled home from the pub. The real St. Peter and the spirit of Genius look on.

> JULIUS: *Shut out! Ha, ha, ha, a Pope shut out of Heaven! That would be a strange Piece of News.*
>
> GENIUS: *Perhaps not so strange as true.*
>
> JULIUS: *What! I warrant you don't see who I am.*
>
> PETER: *See! Yes truly I do see, an odd and uncouth Spectacle, an hideous kind of Monster in my Judgement.*
>
> JULIUS: *Leave your Babbling if you know when you are well; I am not to be trifled with. And if you are so dull as to want Information, know that I am the thrice renown'd Julius, whom Liguria had the honour to produce. And for your satisfaction, view these embroidered letters, S.P.H.F, if ever you learned your A,B,C. From these you may gather my Title and honourable Place. You can't be so stupid as not to know their Meaning.*
>
> PETER: *Tis probable those Letters may stand for, Simoniacal, Pestilent, Horrid, Fellow.*
>
> GENIUS: *Ha, ha, ha. How exactly he has hit the Nail on the Head!*
>
> JULIUS: *No Sauce-box, they stand for Supreme, Pontifical, Holy, Father.*
>
> PETER: *Prodigious! The more I look the more I am*

*amazed, how little of the Apostolick Pastor is to be
discern'd! What's the meaning of that preposterous
Garb, Sacerdotal Habiliments on the outside, and under
those, bloody Weapons and rattling Armour! What
mean those fell Eyes, that domineering Aspect, that
menacing Brow? To my shame and grief I speak it,
there is no one Part about you but exhibits a plain
Indication of a most profligate Ruffian. Ev'n at this
present Time your Hiccups and Belching betray your
riotous courses; nay, if I am not mistaken, I but just
now saw you spewing. Out you Beast!*

Once a year in Nagasaki Harbor, a little later in the
sixteenth century, a cry would go up: "The Great Ships
are coming! The Great Ships are coming!" These heavily
loaded Portuguese galleons from Macao that arrived an-
nually at Nagasaki carried supplies for the Jesuit missionaries. The Japanese regarded the massive oceangoing care
packages with awe, and they painted them in the famous
namban byobu, the "Southern-barbarian screens" which
were later to become such sought-after collector's items.
In order to finance their activities, the Jesuits had found
it necessary to enter trade themselves. The Great Ships
bearing a cargo of silver and gold and precious silk from
the preceding ports of call in the new Christian empire
became a gorgeous bait with which to lure the local lords
and *Daimos.* Even those who had previously been reluctant
to allow the *gaijin* priests into their villages now realized
that the traders and the missionaries were two faces of the

same rich foreign beast. The southern *Daimos* began inviting the Jesuits into their kingdoms in the hope of attracting the Portuguese merchants as well.

A Jesuit Vicar-General, Alessandro Valignano, at over six feet probably the tallest foreigner to be seen in Japan up to then, wrote to his superior, "Your Reverence must understand that after the grace and favor of God the greatest help that we have hitherto had in securing Christians is that of the Great Ships."

The conversion of Japan was proving so successful that it was decided, in 1582, to send a mission of Japanese envoys to Rome to pay homage to the pope. Three of the most powerful of the Christian *Daimos* were approached, and they were delighted to select their own relatives for the journey. They had to be young, for it was an arduous voyage. And of course they had to be baptized. They chose Michael Cingiva, Mantius Ito, Julian Nacaura, and Martin Hara. On February 20, 1582, the envoys, accompanied by several Jesuits, embarked upon a Portuguese vessel at Nagasaki, which the Jesuit bullion dealers had made their headquarters.

On the way across to China the envoy's boat was battered by a cyclone, or, as the locals called it, a *kamikaze,* that lasted five days. They survived it and arrived in Macao only to find that the next vessel sailing for India was not due for another nine months. There were further long delays in Malacca and in Goa. The Japanese envoys spent the time learning Latin and the writing of the West. Their ship was savaged by more storms and attacked by pirates. Finally, after two and a half years, it rounded the

Cape of Good Hope and by August 10, 1584, the four Japanese were in Lisbon. On March 22 of the following year, they arrived at the gates of the Eternal City for their audience with the pope, three years and thirty-two days after setting off from Nagasaki, the first Japanese ever to set foot in Europe.

In Rome, an *envoy-boomu* gripped the populace. The normally cynical locals turned out in their thousands to catch a glimpse of these exotic foreigners. The Japanese wore white silk coats, embroidered in gold with birds and flowers in various colors. In their right hands they carried splendid scimitars, and in their left daggers, their sheaths adorned with lacquer.

Their address to the pope was delivered in Latin by the Portuguese Jesuit Consalvi: "The island kingdom of Japan is, it is true, so far away that its name is hardly known, and some have doubted its very existence. In spite of this, those who know it set it before all the countries of the East, and compare it to those of the West in its size, the number of its cities, and its warlike and cultured people. All that has been lacking to it has been the light of the Christian faith."

The envoys gave Gregory XIII a precious writing desk of ebony as well as a painted screen in the Kano school style, showing the town of Azuchi. It was the first pure landscape ever to be seen in the West. Gregory XIII gave them a gift of 1,000 *scudi* and some European clothes, for it seems that their strange Japanese dress had "excited too much comment among the satirical Roman populace." The first Japanese ever to be forced to wear European clothes made their debut on March 29, 1585, at the granting of indulgences in St. Peter's.

Having beaten so many enemy armies into submission, Julius II then turned his attention to the city of Rome itself, for it was a notoriously chaotic and criminal conurbation. Julius set about imposing order on Rome by meting out a punishment that really hurt: criminals had their houses demolished.

He reorganized the coinage and set up his own papal military unit, a bodyguard he could trust, the Swiss Guards, whose descendants still bar your way to the Bronze Doors of the Vatican today (dressed to kill in a fancy costume allegedly designed by Michelangelo).

Julius was also lucky to live in the era when the great trade routes to the New World were being opened and conquistador gold began to trickle into the Catholic church to help finance the Renaissance. It was Julius who established an archbishopric and the first two bishoprics in the West Indies, in Española (Haiti). Two more followed in Santo Domingo and San Juan, Puerto Rico.

When Columbus died in 1506, the year Michelangelo was first approached to paint the Sistine Chapel ceiling, the religion of the cross had taken the first important steps toward becoming a pancontinental religion. Julius asked that Diego Columbus, the son of "the great discoverer who had done so much to enlarge the sphere of husbandry of the church," was to be treated with special favor by the Spanish court. In 1512, the year Michelangelo completed the Sistine ceiling, the first envoys from the Congo arrived in Rome.

Julius's short, frenetic reign, in which so much happened, ended on the night of February 20, 1513. He was suffering from the fever, and the fashionable quacks into whose hands Roman medicine was entrusted prescribed a solution of gold for him to drink. The golden water was to be Il Terribile's last pleasure. His reign seemed to have rooted in it so much future good and so much future evil. It was Julius II who issued the dispensation that enabled Henry VIII to marry his brother's widow, Catherine of Aragon. Julius was well enough disposed toward the English monarchy because Henry VII had sent him tin from the Cornish mines for the roof of a new cathedral. To thank the English king for his gift of tin, Julius sent him back an offering of Parmesan cheese. In the single most outrageous decision of his reign, Julius had started to build the new cathedral on the site of the old St. Peter's. Knocking down the Christian church that had stood on this sacred spot for over a thousand years was an act either of breathtaking courage, or of remarkable arrogance.

By the time the Japanese envoys completed the return journey to Nagasaki, the fortunes of the Christians in Japan had undergone a serious reversal. It was the arrival in Kyushu of Franciscan and Dominican missionaries that turned the amazing tide of Christian success.

As long as the Jesuits had Japan to themselves all was well. The Jesuits supplied hospitals for the poor and trading contacts for the rich. Their behavior compared favorably with that of the endemic Buddhist priests, whose ruined monasteries had long since become refuges for brigands and vagabonds. The arrival of the Franciscans, Julius II's order, and the preaching Dominicans upset this successful but extremely delicate religious ecosystem. Instead of being in competition only with the forces of paganism, the various religious orders now found themselves in competition with each other as well. The Japanese, who had previously been so impressed by the religious dignity of the southern barbarians, were now treated to the spectacle of various factions of the One True Church squabbling and competing like the very worst Buddhists. The spell was broken.

In 1587 the tyrant Hideyoshi, who had almost completed the unification of the Japanese feudal states, issued a declaration ordering the missionaries to leave, "charging them with forcing Japanese to become Christians, teaching their disciples to wreck temples, eating useful animals and taking slaves to the Indies." The missions were far too well entrenched to obey. They continued to eat useful animals. The order to depart was ignored.

It was the arrival in 1600 of a Dutch ship with an English captain that precipitated the end of the Jesuit empire in Japan. Where the Spanish and Portuguese insisted upon mixing trade with salvation, the Dutch offered goodies without God. The Portuguese and Spanish urged the Japanese warlords to expel the Protestant pirates. The Dutch and the English assured the Japanese that their own countries had waged a long and difficult war with Catholic Spain and that the Spaniards had imperial ambitions: first they conquered your mind with their religion, then they conquered your country with their *tane-gashima teppos*. When a squabble broke out over a Portuguese ship's cargo, the Spanish governor sent Hideyoshi a note of staggering arrogance and insensitivity urging the unifier of Japan to beware: the missionaries always preceded the conquistadors. The Japanese warlords needed little more persuading. Having finally succeeded in unifying their own islands, they did not need the disruptive influence of squabbling and supercilious *gaijins*. Above all they did not want their fledgling nation to become what the Philippines had already become, a vassal state battered into religious and economic servitude by the Spaniards. In 1617 the first Catholic priests were executed. The Dutch, who offered trade without Catholicism, became Japan's main suppliers of Western luxuries.

Back at the gates of heaven, Il Terribile was still trying to bluff his way past St. Peter.

> JULIUS: *Take this for a Maxim, that from the first moment of a Pope's Election, no Vices or Imperfections are to be ascrib'd to him; he immediately becomes Sanctify'd and Infallible, and ought to be look'd upon with Adoration.*
>
> PETER: *What, tho' most notoriously wicked?*
>
> JULIUS: *Ay, tho' as manifestly glaring as the Sun at Noon Day.*
>
> PETER: *Strange. Suppose he murders a man.*

JULIUS: *Tho' he murder'd his own Father, it will not do.*

PETER: *Not for Fornication and Adultery?*

JULIUS: *Ha, ha, ha, you joke. There must be a new Pope every Week, if such Peccadillo's were sufficient for a Removal. No believe me, so insignificant are those Actions that Incest, which is a degree beyond, would signify nothing.*

PETER: *Not for Simoniacal Contract?*

JULIUS: *Not for Ten Thousand.*

In Japan crucifixion had traditionally been considered the most shameful death imaginable, the lowliest form of capital punishment. The Jesuits grasped quickly enough the social horror of crucifixion that transfixed and alienated the law-abiding Japanese. The ubiquitous Christian crucifix played a minor role in the religious conquest of the islands. The Jesuits urged the other orders to remember this. But the Franciscans who arrived in Japan in the 1590s were there to convert, not to understand the specific social niceties of their new hosts. Waving their crucifixes in the faces of the congregation, they encouraged the poor to adopt flagellation and other disgusting practices that the Franciscans favored but which the *Daimos* quite rightly found repulsive and barbaric. When the Spanish governor sent his threatening note to the tyrant Hideyoshi in 1597, Hideyoshi's reply was to crucify twenty-six Christians on a hill overlooking Nagasaki. They went to their deaths singing. From then on it was not enough for the Japanese Christians merely to die for their faith. They were required to apostasize first, to renounce their beliefs and step on a likeness of Christ, a painting or a crucifix.

The Japanese were almost the Chosen People. Conditions could hardly have been more suitable for their successful conversion. The Jesuits were a new order bursting with missionary energy, while Japan was an emerging state with two unconvincing religions, Shinto and Buddhism, that spent more time squabbling among themselves than they did nourishing the spirit. All over the islands only one language was spoken. Had it been completed, the conversion of Japan would have changed the course of world religion. As it was, the Christians failed a crucial test of their judgment. Asked to make the first mature decision of their expansion—to convert through force of will or through force of understanding—they chose the macho route. Having been unable to adapt to a country whose existing social order they failed to understand, the Christian alliance of theologians and tradesmen was now completely unprepared for the force of the anger that was directed at their refusal to leave Japan when told to.

To prolong the agony of Christian victims at the stake, and to give them additional time for reconsideration, a lethal bonfire was placed at some distance from the sufferers so that they could be slowly roasted. The famous Japanese hot springs with their fabled health-giving properties (which John Paul II was later to relax in) supplied the boiling water that was poured slowly over the victims, a dipperful at a time, after slits had first been opened in their flesh. Christians were also tied to stakes at the water's edge at ebb tide so that they drowned slowly as the tide came in. But the cruelest anti-Christian torture was as cruel as anything being employed at exactly the same time in Catholic Madrid by the Spanish Inquisition (which had been accepted and blessed by Julius II's uncle, Sixtus IV). The cruelest of the Nagasaki tortures was as cruel as any torture devised by Cortés and the Spanish conquistadors attempting to bludgeon the Aztecs into Christianity, and steal their gold in the process. The cruelest torture was the Pit. The victim was tied up and suspended upside down over a dark pit. A hole was drilled in his temple. This hole allowed the blood to drip out of the victim's head a splash at a time, thus preventing rapid death from circulatory obstruction. The victim might hang there for as long as a week until the slowly rising blood pressure finally brought about complete exhaustion. Or until he agreed, as the notorious apostate Christopher Ferreira agreed, to step on a likeness of Christ.

In 1637 a rebellion of Christians on the Shimbara Peninsula was ruthlessly put down and a policy of extermination introduced. Japan closed its borders to all foreigners, and they remained comprehensively closed for two centuries. Every year, once a year, until the end of the 1700s, the inhabitants of Nagasaki were required by law to step on the face of Christ.

When John Paul II pronounced the last "Amen" of the interminable three-hour mass in the outdoor sports stadium in Nagasaki that marked the official end of his tour, he had reason to feel satisfied with himself. His meeting with the ex-descendant of the sun-goddess had awakened enough media attention to ensure that his visit was noticed. And he had made an agreement with Yosaij Kobayashi, chairman of the Nippon Television Network Corporation, to sponsor the restoration of the Sistine ceiling. The pop singer and the rock group appearing with him at the final mass had been a tuneful success. And the stadium had been packed despite temperatures that were still way below zero. The Arctic *kamikaze* blowing across Nagasaki from Siberia was so cold that nine communicants had broken bones slipping on the ice during the mass, and 466 members of the congregation had to be treated for exposure. Having once almost been the Chosen People, the Japanese were again exhibiting an impressive commitment to the faith.

It's Christmas Eve. Somewhere deep within the gaslit gloom of Charles Dickens's *Christmas Carol,* Ebenezer Scrooge, that grasping old skinflint, is trying to put on his stockings. Scrooge is having difficulty. He's too old and miserable and impatient to bend well. He struggles mightily with the stockings. This gives Dickens the opportunity to point out Scrooge's uncanny resemblance to Laocoon wrestling with the serpent.

Laocoon was a priest of Troy who tried to stop the Trojans from opening their gates to the Wooden Horse. He and his two sons were then attacked by giant snakes that came out of the sea, probably sent by Apollo, the patron of the Greek invaders cunningly hidden within the Wooden Horse. Virgil gives an account of

Laocoon's death by ophidian coarctation in the second book of the *Aeneid*. The account is memorably bloodthirsty:

"Next they [the snakes] seized Laocoon; they bound him in the giant spirals of their scaly length, twice around his middle, twice round his throat; and still their hands and necks towered above him. His hands strove frantically to wrench the knots apart. Filth and black venom drenched his priestly hands. His shrieks were horrible and filled the sky, like a bull's bellow when an axe has struck awry. . . . "

Sometime around 25 B.C. three sculptors on the island of Rhodes (Agesander, Athenodorus, Polydorus) carved out of marble the almost life-sized scene of Laocoon and his two sons being attacked by the serpent. The statue was brought to Rome by the emperor Titus in A.D. 69, and erected in the Baths of Titus. Much praised by Pliny the Elder, who called it the greatest work of art in the world, the Laocoon presumably persuaded Roman bathers to look twice in the water before dipping a toe. You never know what could be down there. In the *Aeneid,* Laocoon is sacrificing a bull to his sea-god, Neptune, at the very moment that Apollo's snakes rise up from the ocean and slither across the beach of Troy "with blazing and bloodshot eyes and tongues which flickered and licked their hissing mouths. We paled at the sight and scattered; they forged on, straight at Laocoon."

The *Laocoon* is a wide, unwieldy sculpture, three bulky humans and one large snake struggling energetically in a confined space like an old Victorian skinflint putting on his stockings. The tussle between man and snake extends upward as well as sideways, and the statue must have taken some unearthing when Felice de' Freddi discovered it in his vineyard near S. Maria Maggiore on January 14, 1506. Felice spread the word and Pope Julius's architect, Giuliano de Sangallo, was dispatched to have a look at it. Giuliano took his infant son with him, hitched up on his shoulders, and also the pope's new favorite, the Florentine sculptor Michelangelo. Both of them admired the statue deeply. According to Sangallo's son, who published his recollections of the event sixty years later, it was his father who recognized the sculpture immediately as the famous *Laocoon* described by Pliny, which had ornamented the Palace of Titus, "of all paintings and sculpture the most worthy of admiration." Against stiff competition from other Roman collectors of antique art, Julius II exercised his papal muscle and bought the *Laocoon* for the new sculpture garden he had established in the Vatican. When the *Laocoon* was carried through the streets of Rome to its next home, the people threw flowers at it. And the Cappella Giulia, the reputedly magnificent papal choir, also founded by Julius, sang an accompaniment. The *Laocoon* became an artistic archetype, as famous in its time as the fingers of God and Adam up on the Sistine ceiling are in ours. Everybody wanted a copy. The Gonzagas wanted one fashioned in gold. Isabella d'Este ordered a *Laocoon* "cap badge." Flavio Sirletti carved a copy out of amethyst for the Duke of Beaufort.

Not only was Michelangelo one of the first people in modern times to see the *Laocoon*. He was also one of the first to be influenced by it at a nuclear level.

Julius II was a Franciscan, and the Franciscans were instructed by their vows to devote their religious life to the imitation of Christ. Franciscans were expected to give away all their possessions and wander, just as their founder had himself wandered into the ruined chapel of S. Damiano outside Assisi, where he heard the voice of God issuing from a talking crucifix: "Go, Francis, and repair my house, which, as you see, is well nigh in ruins." Francis set himself a task: "to follow the teachings of our Lord Jesus Christ and to walk in his footsteps." In practice this meant imitating the life of Christ so thoroughly that when he died it was discovered that Francis of Assisi had developed secret stigmata, and was bleeding from his hands and feet.

I once visited a nightclub in Tokyo where every single act on the bill attempted an imitation of the Beatles: the same songs, the same clothes, the same hairstyles, the same harmonies, all learned with note-perfect Japanese precision. Of course, the differences were more significant than the similarities, and by the end of the night the Beatles imitations had metamorphosed into peculiarly Japanese hybrids of Moptop Pop. In the same way, the early Toyota cars built in imitation of American models were significantly different from the originals, smaller, more practical, with better fuel consumption. And Japanese baseball, which NTV covers so well, is significantly different from the American version, which was itself a corruption of the English game of rounders. Since the whole of the Japanese economic miracle is built on a foundation of imitation, it is worth noting that the modern Japanese are therefore closer relatives of Renaissance men than modern Italians are. Imitation meant something positive to the Renaissance that it does not mean to the modern West. Not only was it an accepted way of learning and of paying homage to a worthy subject, it was also more than that, more than a fashion: it was an attitude that underpinned the entire economic and social development of the Renaissance.

"It's only sign-painters who would copy the work of others," squealed Gauguin, expressing the typical modern prejudice against imitation, and in the process dismissing Michelangelo as a sign-painter, for Michelangelo was an enthusiastic copyist. (So was Van Gogh, at whom Gauguin's jibe was aimed. Van Gogh said: "In these wretched fine arts all is forgotten, and nothing is kept.") Michelangelo copied in the Renaissance spirit, that is to say in a spirit of learned imitation, as Julius II imitated St. Francis when he too heard some sort of talking crucifix advising him: "Go, Julius, and repair my house, which, as you see, is well nigh in ruins."

Rome was unarguably a dump when Julius II came to power. The woods and copses were so thick within the city walls that hare and deer were hunted in the streets around the Pantheon. Armed gangs roamed the woodland margins, and every morning the bodies of the stabbed were stepped over to be cleaned up—*domani,* perhaps. Three in every hundred women were estimated to be courtesans. As Alberto de' Alberti complained, "The men of the present day, who call themselves Romans, are very different in conduct from the ancient inhabitants. They all look like cowherds."

When Martin Luther came to Rome early in the sixteenth century on business for his order, he was appalled by what he saw: "The old buildings were now buried beneath the new, so deep lieth the rubbish, as is plain to see by the Tiber, since it hath banks of rubbish as high as twice the length of a soldier's spear." Somewhere under the twenty-foot-tall mounds of rubbish was buried Ancient Rome. The ruins that so many generations of visitors would come to adore provided excellent shelter for the various kinds of thieves in whom Rome specialized. Ruins were everywhere; uncared for, overgrown, they disrupted whatever ambitions for town planning an overseer might have had. Punctuated by these huge, smelly semicircles of moldering stumps, Renaissance Rome looked like a decayed mouth. At least the ruins provided excellent building materials for the notoriously lazy Roman populace. And the marbles of the Colosseum made high-quality lime when burned.

In the winter the Roman marshes froze over and became dangerous. In the summer they became a favorite breeding ground of the mosquito. Malaria mingled nicely with the syphilis that Columbus's sailors had brought back from the Americas. Seventeen members of Pope

Alexander VI's family were treated for it, including Cesare Borgia, the pope's bastard son, that fabulously degenerate Renaissance ogre into whose clutches it was best not to fall. Pity the anti-Borgia lampoonist who was captured and who had his tongue and his hand nailed together.

The reign of the Borgia pope Alexander VI, 1492–1503, provides the low-water mark of Rome's religious and temporal well-being. Rival candidates lived in fortified palaces and had crossbowmen sitting in the windows (just as crossbowmen had a special gallery built for them on the roof of the fortified Sistine Chapel). Alexander took the art of papal nepotism to spectacular new heights. His favorite bastard daughter, the poisonous Lucretia, rode through the Vatican on a bejeweled horse, and in 1500, the Holy Year, she had her second husband stabbed on the steps of St. Peter's. A more profitable marriage awaited her. Cesare Borgia sat on horseback on these same steps of St. Peter's and threw lances at bulls gathered in wooden enclosures in the piazza. Then he cut their heads off.

There were floods and pox. The Tiber was brown with sewage. The Catholic church was in ruins, financially, spiritually, geographically. There was only one functioning aqueduct still supplying fresh water to the capital of Christendom. It was Roman, of course, a stone umbilical cord still linking the Renaissance to its great and glorious urban past. Alexander VI's successor, Pius III, died ten days after his coronation. The new century was only three years old when Julius II became pope. In imitation of St. Francis, whose vows he had repeated, he set about rebuilding the church. In imitation of Julius Caesar, whose name he took, he set about rebuilding Rome.

"Only now do I begin to live," noted an enthusiastic Goethe on his arrival in Rome in 1786. "I have not spent an entirely happy day since I crossed the Ponte Molle to come home," he complained later, on his return to Germany. The power of Rome to take root in the imaginations of men and grow into something huge and largely unconnected with the real city cannot easily be explained. Certainly it has never been a cheap city, or a friendly one, or particularly safe, relaxing, comfortable, cool, or private. Under the Borgias the physician of the Hospital of the Lateran used to shoot passersby with a crossbow. Rich patients who confessed their wealth to the hospital confessor were poisoned. When a man murdered his two daughters in the reign of Innocent X he was allowed to purchase his freedom for eight hundred ducats. The vice-chamberlain explained: "Rather than the death of a sinner, God wishes that he should live—and pay!" It is a policy by which the hoteliers of Rome still seem to govern their lives today.

Rome has two sets of tenants: the Romans who actually live there and who have been inventively preying on pilgrims in one way or another since the Dark Ages, and the pilgrims themselves, who have been coming from all over the world, West and East, since classical times, in search of a city they have already discovered in their imaginations. Rome was lived in by the locals but built in the dreams of visitors. It was Bramante (from Fermignano) who designed the new basilica of St. Peter's, for which Julius II (from Liguria) laid the white marble foundation stone in 1506, dropping it into a hole twenty-five feet deep. It was Raphael (from Urbino) who painted the new papal apartments that Julius moved to when he could no longer bear to live in the apartments left to him by the hated Alexander VI (born Rodrigo de Borja y Borja, in Valencia, Spain). It was Bramante again who designed the sculpture court that Julius built in front of the Vatican's Belvedere pavilion, in imitation of the Romans, filled with classical statuary and surrounded by sweet-smelling orange groves, the first pleasure garden to be built in Rome since the time of the emperors. It was Michelangelo (from Florence) who was called to Rome to carve Julius's funeral monument and later to paint the Sistine ceiling. It was Giuliano da Sangallo (also from Florence) who helped Michelangelo cure the mold that disrupted work on the Sistine ceiling in 1509; Giuliano also identified the *Laocoon* that ended up in Bramante's sculpture garden, along with the famous *Apollo Belvedere* and the *Hercules and Antaeus* that Thomas Jefferson (from Shadwell, Virginia) hoped to include among the sculptures in the art gallery he wanted to build in Monticello in 1771, in imitation of Julius II. It was Goethe (from Frankfurt-am-Main) who wrote the finest essay on the *Laocoon.* And Charles Dickens (from Portsea and London) who arrived in Rome in 1844 and expressed the biggest disappointment at what he saw. He had imagined a city of ruins and at first he thought he had found it: "We had crossed the Tiber by the Ponte Molle, two or three miles before. It had looked as yellow as it ought to look, and hurrying between its worn-away and miry banks, had a promising aspect of desolation and ruin." But disappointment lay in store for Dickens. Passing through the Porta del Popolo, he discovered civilization: "There were no ruins, no solemn tokens of antiquity, to be seen. There seemed to be long streets of commonplace shops and houses, such as are to be found in any European town; there were busy people, equipages, ordinary walkers to and fro; a multitude of chattering strangers. It was no more *my* Rome: the Rome of anybody's fancy, man or boy: degraded and fallen and lying asleep in the sun among a heap of ruins. . . . " Dickens had come in search of an imaginary crumbling Rome that bore some resemblance to the Rome that Julius II had actually inherited, the Rome which Savonarola (from Ferrara) described as a sink of iniquity. It was Mussolini (from Predappio, in the province of Forli) who drove the overwide Via della Conciliazione through the cluttered old streets of the Vatican while earlier on in the century Michelangelo's house in the street known as the Macel de' Corvi at the foot of the Capitoline Hill was demolished to make way for the monument to Victor Emmanuel II (from Turin), the unifier of Italy. On every Easter Sunday, even during the reign of the Borgias, two hundred thousand worshippers (from the whole world over) have knelt in the square in front of St. Peter's and awaited the papal blessing. The audience was there for a rebuilt church. And in Julius II the church found an inveterate rebuilder.

Michelangelo was twenty-one years old when he arrived in Rome for the first time in 1496. Rodrigo de Borja y Borja (Alexander VI) was in the middle of the most corrupt pontificate in papal history and Giuliano della Rovere, a loud opponent of the Borgias, was in exile. Michelangelo was professionally trained in painting, having worked with Ghirlandaio, a fact he later tried to conceal, as we have seen. His first biographers also insist that he had already carved a *Sleeping Cupid* so convincingly worked in the manner of the ancients that a Roman merchant had bought and sold it as a genuine classical antique. Cardinal Riaria, a relative of the Rovere popes, was so impressed by this fake *Cupid* that he invited the young Michelangelo to Rome, apparently to study in his palace, where he had organized a school or academy of art in imitation of the one in Florence set up by Lorenzo de' Medici, where Michelangelo, according to Condivi and Vasari, had begun his education as a sculptor.

This extraordinary story of the fake *Sleeping Cupid* that fooled the experts must surely be seen as another embellishment of the Michelangelo myth, an exaggeration if not a complete fabrication. But Michelangelo lies are just as revealing as Michelangelo truths. The *Sleeping Cupid* features proudly in Michelangelo's earliest biographies not as it would appear to us—as a sign of his dishonesty and lack of originality—but as it must have appeared to his Renaissance peers—as amazing proof of his proficiency. Vasari goes even further in his praise of Michelangelo the counterfeiter: "He also forged sheets by the hands of various old masters with such similitude that no one recognized it; for he tinged and aged them with smoke and various other means, and so dirtied them that they looked old and, when compared with the originals, they could not be distinguished from them: and he did this so that, by giving his copies he might retain the originals for himself."

Michelangelo, the precocious genius who was privy to the secrets and skills of the ancients, was soon in demand in Rome. Cardinal Riaria's next-door neighbor, Jacopo Galli, commissioned a *Bacchus* from him to stand in the sculpture garden that he too had set up in imitation of the ancients. Of all Michelangelo's completed works, this drunken *Bacchus,* nude, open-mouthed, and swaying, has drawn the most criticism from unimpressed modern observers. Shelley opined, "The countenance of this figure is the most revolting mistake of the spirit and meaning of Bacchus. It looks drunken, brutal, and narrow-minded, and has an expression of dissoluteness the most revolting."

Revolting or not, Michelangelo's *Bacchus* stood in Jacopo Galli's sculpture garden looking convincingly ancient, and for much of the sixteenth century it even had a hand missing, presumably knocked off deliberately so that the *Bacchus* might appear classically ruined. The great Portuguese braggart Francisco da Holanda, who wrote an amusing dialogue in which he features himself discussing matters of the highest artistic importance with Michelangelo (even though the two probably never met), makes a point of boasting that he, Francisco da Holanda, friend of Michelangelo, was not fooled and immediately recognized the *Bacchus* as a contemporary work. Since Francis-

co's description of the *Bacchus* is characteristically inac-
curate in descriptive details, it seems fair to assume that
once again in this most imaginative of centuries, we are
being presented with fantasy tastefully disguised as fact.
Da Holanda seems to have heard of the *Bacchus,* but not
to have seen it.

The *Laocoon* still stands in the Vatican's Belvedere
courtyard, where it has stood for four hundred and fifty
years, an old man and his two sons wrestling with a giant
snake, like a Victorian novelist struggling with a giant
simile. It is not difficult to see the unbreakable attraction
of this ancient wrestling match. The *Laocoon,* unlike the
Apollo Belvedere in the next niche along, which also stood
in Julius's sculpture garden, has never fallen out of favor
or fashion. It is the archetypal image of struggle. It is not
just Scrooge with his stockings, but anyone who has ever
struggled with anything, physically or spiritually, who is
tempted to invoke the *Laocoon,* a splendid sculptural met-
aphor waiting to be cited.

Goethe wrote an essay on the *Laocoon,* in which he
advised: "To seize well the attention of the Laocoon, let
us place ourselves before the group with our eyes shut,
and at the necessary distance, let us open and shut them
alternately, and we shall see all the marble in motion; we
shall be afraid to find the group changed when we open
our eyes again. I would readily say, as the group is now
exposed, it is a flash of lightning fixed, a wave petrified
at the instant when it is approaching the shore. We see
the same effect when we see the group at night, by the

light of flambeaux." Goethe planned an essay on viewing statues by torchlight. It was flambeaux like his that turned the Sistine fresco black.

In imitation of Goethe, I tried to do what he did and stood before the *Laocoon* alternately opening and shutting my eyes. As a child of the movie century I could hardly be as impressed as he was by the visual jerking that indeed takes place. But Goethe's crude protocinematic technique is revealing. And since the judo-trained Vatican guards no longer allow you to enter the museum with a torch, I thoroughly recommend all viewers of the *Laocoon* to imitate Goethe and me and to stand before the statue, blinking madly. "One of the greatest merits of this monument," continued Goethe in his essay, "is the moment which the artist has represented." Looked at stroboscopically, the *Laocoon* is clearly seen to be a sculpture pregnant with movement. It is this protocinematic sense of a moment frozen, of an action about to happen, that Michelangelo discovered in the vineyard of Felice de' Freddi and carried with him up onto the scaffolding of the Sistine ceiling.

THE ARGUMENT

I went to Rome in 1988 not because I was sent by my king as da Holanda had been, but because I wanted to witness what the professor of fine art at New York University, Sir John Pope-Hennessy (in an article in the *New York Review of Books*), had called the single most important art event of the century, the restoration of the Sistine ceiling. As it happened, I did not believe in the existence of genius. I believed in greatness as a human condition that could be arrived at after much hard work and the energetic deployment of talent. I believed that one artist could achieve more than another in the same way that Boris Becker is a considerably better tennis player than others around him. But I did not believe in genius as a shortcut to this achievement. I did not believe in the myth of an artist

WITH LOUD
APOLOGIES TO
FRANCISCO DA
HOLANDA

who arrives at greatness because of some sort of quasi-divine topping up of his talent. I say "his" talent because you must have noticed how few female geniuses have been recognized. All these Einsteins and Leonardos and Michelangelos are old, male, bearded, and biblical, super-clever grandfathers who put the human race on their knee and pat it on the head: "There, there. Don't worry about what you don't know. Grandpa's here." In my book, geniuses are there for the same reason as the yeti, the Loch Ness Monster, and little green men. I went to Rome in search of Michelangelo's humanity. It was my belief that the correct way to view his achievements was to see them as magnificently tellurian ones.

But Italians hate being told they don't know something about other Italians. Sixty feet above the Sistine floor, after another unwanted Turkish bath caused by another boiling-hot Roman morning, I was finally forced to accept that the three wise Vatican restorers would always remain stubbornly resistant to my views. It was time to come down in that phutt, phutt, phutting elevator. I needed to find some way to take my mind off the convoluted case history of the Sistine ceiling and decided to spend the afternoon doing what Rome is certainly not made for—walking. Whoever said Rome was built on seven hills couldn't count. Down the Lungo Tevere Michelangelo I hurried to take a peep into the ritzy car emporium that I admired twice daily on my journeys to and from the Vatican. What was it to be today, vice or virtue, the Ferrari or the BMW? I chose vice as always, but the promise of the Ferrari failed to cheer me up.

Continuing south along the Tiber-walk to the Piazza della Rovere I cupped some water in my hands from the fountain on the corner and splashed my hot head. Somehow today the Della Rovere water failed to cool me down. Straight along the Lungo Tevere Raffaelo Sanzio I marched, across the Ponte Fabricio to the Capitoline, "much more of a mole-hill than a mountain," said Henry James, who presumably never tried to climb it at twelve noon in August. Neither did I that day, preferring to skirt around the base where Michelangelo's house used to be in the Macel de' Corvi, the Market of the Crows, before the city's brutal urban planners decided to swop all those sweet small crows for one ugly gargantuan monument to Victor Emmanuel II. I found myself in the Forum at an ancient Roman crossroads: To the right was the Colosseum, which Henry James called the Moby Dick of architecture because it stands for so many big and white and submerged hopes. Edgar Allan Poe, who never went to Rome, imagined that he knew the Colosseum well: "Where once there were eagles, gilded hair and monarchs, there are now bats, thistles, and lizards," he complained. Even the bats and the thistles are gone today. All that remains is the noonday sun ripening the tourists nicely. Anyway I wasn't interested in virtuous ruins so I veered left at Trajan's Column, up the Via Ventiquattro, and soon I was turning left again into the little church of S. Silvestro al Quirinale where the vice of sloth beckoned, and where I hoped to take a nap.

The terrace of S. Silvestro looks out across Rome and provides a splendid aerial view of the Eternal City. In the

courtyard under a shady laurel tree is a stone bench, a
perfect spot for sitting, reading a guidebook, or snoozing.
Michelangelo's friend Vittoria Colonna, the Marchesa de
Pescara, would meet here with various Catholic intellectuals and talk. It was here too that the preposterous
Portuguese braggart Francisco da Holanda set the notorious *Dialogues* in which he imagined himself encountering
Vittoria Colonna and Michelangelo in this very courtyard
one Sunday afternoon, and striking up a conversation with
them about art and its meaning. The Portuguese fop was
an entertaining fraud, but at least he was lucky enough
to find a seat. It so happened that on this particular
lunchtime the stone bench was already occupied by an
elderly couple, sitting upright, staring at me as I came
through the gate. He was sporting a thick white beard,
neatly trimmed, and wearing a green corduroy jacket that
had leather patches on the elbows (very similar to one my
grandfather used to wear). She was a nun, all in white. I
recognized her immediately as the Polish nun I had seen
earlier in the week taking a party of her country's pilgrims
around the Vatican museums, rushing them past the *Laocoon,* past the *Apollo Belvedere,* past a museumload of celebrated classical treasures before finally coming to a halt
in front of a simple marble bath, which had once been
Roman but which the Christians had turned into a font.
The nun then informed her Polish flock of how much this
gimmicky marble font weighed. They had been impressed. I wasn't. How could anyone rush past the *Laocoon?*
There was room on the bench for one more, so I waved
an apology, and made sure I shuffled in next to the old

man. There we were, the three of us, happy as monkeys, sitting underneath a shady laurel tree, looking out over the Eternal City, seeing no evil, hearing no evil, speaking no evil, grunting with pleasure.

"Booz," exclaimed the old man again, reaching across and patting my knee. It wasn't a grunt of pleasure after all.

"Excuse me, sir?" I gabbled back.

"You were thinking of Booz, the old husband of Ruth, painted by Michelangelo in the Sistine Chapel," he elaborated.

The look of wild amazement on my face would not have seemed out of place on the end of a Fool's stick. At that very moment I had indeed been imagining the sad old patriarch up on the Sistine walls, wondering once again why Michelangelo had decided to paint him as an imbecile.

"You see, you were testing out a rather silly expression as you daydreamed, slightly opening your mouth and thrusting your chin forward. There's no need to look so embarrassed now. Your movements were minimal. Most observers would not have made much of them. But I have trained myself to notice the smallest facial contortion and to understand its physiognomic significance. What is more, your hands were opening and closing on your lap as if they were trying out a particular kind of grip. This confirmed what I had suspected from the moment you stepped into this courtyard. It was the binoculars hanging over your shoulder that first alerted me to your true mission. Either you were a bird-watcher who had wandered way off course"—he chuckled at this—"or you were carrying the binoculars in order to look at frescoes hidden high up on the church roofs of Rome. The latter was clearly the more likely explanation, given the circumstances of your arrival here. Not many casual visitors stumble across this church. It is somewhat out of the way. Those visitors who cannot be described as casual and who have traipsed up here for a purpose are almost invariably drawn by the Michelangelo connection. This, after all, is the very courtyard in which the Portuguese aesthetician, Francisco da Holanda, set his celebrated 'Dialogue' between himself, Vittoria Colonna, and Michelangelo. I knew from the moment you walked in that you had been here before, because you were looking down at the ground as you entered the gate and not ahead of you, or into a guidebook, which is what you would undoubtedly have been doing had this been your first visit. You knew where you were going. And I thought I knew immediately where you had come from. I recognized that hefty picture volume poking out of your shoulder bag. It has been brought out jointly by the Japanese television company, NTV—who, I believe, are usually makers of soap operas and quiz shows—and the Vatican, and it deals with the restoration of the Sistine ceiling. That volume weighs just over two pounds—I also have a copy—and no one in their right senses would carry it about with them in this heat unless they absolutely had to, or unless they had just bought it. Your copy, I see, is well thumbed, rather battered, in fact, so the chances were that you were carrying it because it was constantly in use. What I had thus learned about

you already from this first appraisal was that you were an
aficionado of art who was interested in Michelangelo, who
had been here before, and who had probably just visited
the Sistine Chapel. Since at this time of year it closes at
twelve-thirty and it is now one-forty-one, I surmised further that you had walked here from the Vatican, hence
your rather, er, sweaty aroma. No, don't move. To come
to Rome and not to sweat—that would be something out
of the ordinary. But, to continue with our observations,
what, I asked myself, were you doing here? When you
looked up and saw the two of us sitting on this bench, a
tiny scowl of disappointment tweaked the corners of your
mouth. You had probably wanted to be alone. Perhaps to
take a snooze, as I myself am fond of doing at this time
of day. But when you noticed us, it was me that you
stared at the longest. This was curious. Most people would
have stared at Sister Korona here. She, after all, presents
the more interesting spectacle in her brilliantly gleaming
habit, as white as Noah's dove. What is it about me that
could have interested you? I am of average appearance. It
was most unlikely that you had ever seen me before, as I
live here in Rome in almost complete seclusion and you
are definitely not an Italian. It was much more probable
that I reminded you of someone, or represented to you a
type you were interested in. The most obvious distinguishing feature concerning my person that can be noted
from the first glimpse is that I am an old man with a
beard. When you came and sat down next to me, even
though there was more room next to Sister Korona here,
I could only assume that there was a reason for your choice,

subconscious perhaps, but a reason nevertheless. As you swiveled to sit down, you almost hit me with the heavy shoulder bag that you swung to the ground—no, don't apologize, it's easy to do. Before I ducked I saw clearly that your book on the Sistine Chapel had a marker sticking out of it. The marker, incidentally, was a ticket for the Vatican museum, carrying today's color and thereby confirming all that I had so far surmised for myself. As I said, I too own this book, and although not even I could tell from a glimpse exactly what page in a closed book you had marked, I could see that it was that part of the volume near the end which deals with the restoration of the Sistine lunettes. When your hands started flexing themselves as if trying out an imaginary grip on a finger exerciser, I examined these muscular actions out of the corner of my eye and decided that they corresponded to the movements of someone holding something in front of them, a mirror handle, or the shaft of a walking stick. There are only two figures among the three hundred thirty or so in the Sistine fresco that hold something in front of them in this manner. Both, as it happens, are to be found among the ancestors of Christ featured in the lunettes. One is a young woman who gazes into a mirror and who perhaps represents the vice of Vanity. The other is old Booz staring at his own likeness carved in the handle of his Fool's stick. Booz probably represents the vice of Folly. When I saw you pushing your chin out and opening your mouth, and I remembered the interested look you had given me when you walked into the courtyard, I could hardly fail but come to the conclusion that at that very moment you were thinking of old Booz up on the Sistine walls. So I interrupted your ruminations by pronouncing his name."

By the time this old-timer had finished his soliloquy, my lower lip had drooped down to somewhere around my sandals. No man likes to think of himself as such a flagrantly open book.

"Allow me to introduce myself," continued my remarkable bench-mate, chuckling at my evident discomfort. "My name is Professor Edgar Zephyr. If you are the Michelangelo aficionado I think you are, then you may be familiar with my book, *Mysterious Pagans in the Renaissance.* This"—he gestured toward the nun in white—"is Sister Wiktorja Korona, who is attached to the Polish delegation at the Vatican. I am a historian and an amateur painter. She is a Marian sister and a poet." Sister Korona reached out her hand, and I took it, not knowing whether I should kneel before her and kiss it or what. Still trembling, I settled for a rather bloodless squeeze and shake. She had a hand like Andy Warhol's, very bony.

"Was my old friend correct in his inferences?" she asked, in a heavy accent that sounded like a fat man running across gravel. "He usually is."

"Indeed he was, in every single detail, Sister," I lied, for I could hardly tell her the real reason why I had sat down next to him rather than her. "I have come here straight from seeing the Sistine ceiling and I was hoping that the delightful ambiance of San Silvestro, which I know well, would inspire me to understand more fully that complicated and infuriating masterpiece. Professor

Zephyr is absolutely right. I was thinking of old Booz. You see, it seems to me that the caricature of Booz is one of the keys to the understanding of the entire ceiling. It is one of the few figures in which Michelangelo shows his hand as a symbolist. As you know, you could fill a library many times over with the books that have been written about Michelangelo and the Sistine ceiling, but no one to my knowledge has satisfactorily explained the meaning of the ceiling as a whole. Thousands have, of course, tried. But for every agreement there are ten thousand disagreements. Scholars cannot even agree if the design of the ceiling is Michelangelo's own work or the work of some learned theologian in the circle of Julius the Second. What then did Michelangelo mean when he wrote to his friend Giovanni Francesco Fatucci in December, 1523, that fifteen years earlier Julius the Second had given him 'a new commission to do what I liked' on the Sistine ceiling? Are we to take this literally? Is the fresco entirely Michelangelo's invention? If so, that would be something of a Renaissance first, wouldn't it—a pope allowing an untried young painter to do whatever he wanted on the roof of the most important chapel in Christendom? We know that Julius originally wanted Michelangelo to paint the Twelve Apostles on the vault. There is even a drawing of this first scheme in the British Museum that indicates the original plan for twelve figures surmounted by an expanse of illusionistic ceiling. Who changed the pope's mind about the apostles and who persuaded him to go for something more ambitious? Was it—"

"Oh, yes, yes. I do remember." Sister Korona interrupted me with a shower of verbal gravel. "I saw the film with Charlton Heston that told the whole story exactly as it happened. Michelangelo is painting the Twelve Apostles, but nothing is going right for him. 'I don't mock them,' he says to his girlfriend, Contessina de' Medici, played by Audrey Hepburn, I think. 'They mock me. All twelve of them.' No, it wasn't Audrey Hepburn. It was Sophia Loren. Anyway, to drown his sorrows he goes to the local tavern and orders wine. When the servant girl brings him the wine, he spits it out. 'This wine is sour,' he shouts. The tavernkeeper tastes the wine and he too spits it out. Then the tavernkeeper uncorks the barrel in which the wine is kept and allows the whole lot to spill out across the tavern floor. 'If the wine is sour,' he yells at all the drinkers in the tavern, 'then pour it out.' So Michelangelo goes back up onto the scaffolding. And he starts destroying the Apostles he has painted. All the time he is muttering to himself, 'If the wine is sour, pour it out.'"

"Actually, it wasn't Audrey Hepburn or Sophia Loren who played Contessina de' Medici. It was Diane Cilento." The three of us looked up in unison, like one body with three heads. In the middle of the courtyard stood a gaunt middle-aged American with a cigar. He had come in very quietly, quite an achievement given the gaudiness of his jacket, which was a Rothkoish affair in purple, yellow, and red. "Sorry to interrupt. But I couldn't let a movie mistake like that go unchallenged. Quite what Diane Cilento was doing in the film only the scriptwriter knows. If anyone was going to supply the love interest, it should surely have been Vittoria Colonna. In any case, since Michelangelo was homosexual, the female love interest was phony. Of course, Heston makes no mention of Michelangelo's homosexuality in his memoirs. Incidentally, on the subject of Hollywood and its treatment of artists, have you heard the Van Gogh story Kirk Douglas tells in his autobiography? It seems that after the dinner party arranged to celebrate the successful release of *Lust for Life,* Douglas and John Wayne went for an evening stroll along the terrace. Suddenly Wayne turned angrily to Douglas and roared: 'Christ, Kirk! How can you play a part like that? There's so goddam few of us left. We got to play strong, tough characters. Not those weak queers.' That was the end of a beautiful friendship between Kirk and John. Let me introduce myself. The name's Blueberg. Derwent Blueberg. I write about art."

"Derwent Blueberg!" I exclaimed. "Author of *Expressionist Abstraction* and *How I Busted the Man Who Busted Geometry?*"

"That's me."

We all introduced ourselves again, and Sister Korona moved up to allow Blueberg to squeeze in. When the four of us had settled, Professor Zephyr was the first to speak, turning to me: "I am interested in your interest in Booz. From my own observations of the Sistine frescoes I would conclude that Booz is that most typical of Neoplatonic heroes, the bittersweet lover. When I say bittersweet I mean it in the sense that Sappho meant it, the sense of γλυκύπικρον. The general conceit being that a great love is also a great death. That is also the sense that

Aristophanes intended to convey when he wrote in *The Birds*: 'Of darkness an egg, from the whirlwind conceived, / was laid by the sable-plumed Night, / And out of that egg, as the seasons revolved, / sprang love, the entrancing, the bright.' Just as the egg came out of the darkness, so old Booz meets young Ruth, who illuminates his old age. They fall in love and marry. What a Neoplatonist like Ficino or Pico della Mirandola would have made of this story was that Booz's happiness at getting a young woman should be seen as a prefiguration of his death. Which in itself was, of course, a symbol of his ultimate regeneration, because Booz, like all the ancestors, prefigures Christ. You will remember that in the *Hypnerotomachia* the Great Jupiter blesses Amor in these very words: 'σύ μοί γλυκύς τε καὶ πικρός.' Which means, as I know you know, 'You are sweet for me and bitter.' Thus Booz's happiness and his unhappiness become one and the same thing. His Love becomes his Death. Which is why Michelangelo has deliberately confused the meaning of Booz's bauble stick on which his own likeness is carved. The obvious way to read it is as a Fool's stick, in which case Booz looking at himself represents Folly. But if you were to read it is as a mirror in which Booz is examining his own likeness then it could be taken to symbolize Prudence. Since Folly and Prudence are the vices and virtues that traditionally oppose each other, Michelangelo by putting them together had deliberately—"

"Oh do shut up, Zephyr. You haven't a clue what you're talking about. And neither does anyone else on this bench. You've been spouting this Neoplatonic drivel for the best part of half a century, and, quite frankly, I am sick to my undergarments of it. It's just an excuse to show off your Greek, you vain old billy goat. You are not helping anyone understand anything."

This extraordinary outburst from Sister Korona immediately silenced our merry company. That wiry woman leaned across and pinched the good Professor Zephyr in the ear as if he were a naughty schoolboy. We all fell into nervous quietude. I for one regretted that in silencing Zephyr and ridiculing his methods we were denying ourselves a valuable source of understanding. I ventured to inform the miserable company of my feelings.

"I think it would be foolish on our parts to dismiss entirely what Professor Zephyr has just said purely on the strength of religious intolerance's prejudice against modern learning. I know the Neoplatonists have talked themselves purple in the face in their attempt to understand the Sistine fresco and that they have sometimes—not to make too fine a point of it—cocked things up mightily. I am thinking of Professor Carl Tolgate's assertion, made thirty years ago, that Michelangelo was employing color symbolism in the chapel, that the lunettes represent the lower, darker world of mortals, while the ceiling represents the altogether higher world of the gods. As you know, it has since turned out that the lunettes were merely considerably more dirty than the ceiling because they had not been cleaned since they were painted. But let us not forget that the young Michelangelo was undoubtedly attached to the household of Lorenzo de' Medici and that he worked for a time in the academy, or school, that Lorenzo had set up in Florence in imitation of the ancients. It is inconceivable—despite the fact that he seems not to have spoken Latin—that the boy Michelangelo would not have absorbed some of the Neoplatonic learning that we know to have been current in Lorenzo's court in the circle of Ficino and Pico. How else can we understand the fondness for puns and cleverly hidden meanings that he later displays in his work, notably in his poems? For instance, the sonnet which Professor Zephyr must know in which Michelangelo compares an old man falling in love to some dry sticks being thrown on a bonfire: "That man who scoffs and says there should be shame / When old men love—that man profanes and lies. / It is no sin when human creatures dream / Of natural loveliness; no sins arise / As long as prudence keeps its sovereign claim." Prudence, as we know, is usually represented by a figure staring at its own likeness in a mirror. Can we use this as evidence to support Zephyr's clever suggestion that Michelangelo, by showing Booz gazing into his own face on a Fool's stick, was intending to indicate Prudence safeguarding an old man's love rather than Folly mocking it? Perhaps he was cheekily attempting a Neoplatonic double-entendre that united vice with virtue, which would also by typical of the man. What is certain is that by painting Booz as he did, Michelangelo was not intending to be rude about Booz's appearance or insulting about his sexual ambitions, which is how it might appear to ignorant modern audiences. Whichever way you look at Booz, he was clearly painted as a symbol. Michelangelo was a typ-

ical Renaissance intellectual who enjoyed mixing fantasy
and fact just as that pompous Portuguese da Holanda did
when he set his imaginary 'Dialogue' with Vittoria Colonna in this very courtyard."

Sister Korona, who had been listening to my attack
on her attack on Zephyr with mounting ill humor, could
contain herself no longer: "You asinine, pig-ignorant,
braying, cloth-eared, arrogant atheist of a devil, you," she
spluttered, for words like "asinine" cannot issue freely
from Polish lips without a considerable amount of lubri-
cation. "How typical of the Satan of learning not even to
consider the most fundamental of all truths about Michelangelo: that he was a deeply and sincerely religious
man. Explain to me with your neononsensical Plato-pap
what Michelangelo was attempting to symbolize when he
represented himself as Nicodemus in the late *Pietà* in the
cathedral museum in Florence. Here is an old man waiting
for death. That is all. You can see that death mirrored in
his eyes. Or are we to assume that the beard around his
mouth is in fact alluding to the vice of not shaving? And
that his broken nose should be seen as an allegory of
pugilism? What, pray, was Michelangelo attempting to
reveal beyond the simple religious facts of the Holy Moth-
er's love for Christ when he carved the youthful *Pietà* that
still stands in St. Peter's? Hidden today, regrettably, behind hammerproof glass. It was finished, as you know,
during his first visit to Rome, long before your ludicrous
Laocoon was dug up out of the ground . . . "

How did she know about the *Laocoon*? I had not said

a word on the subject. I had done nothing to suggest I had seen her brush past it.

" . . . long before the limp-wristed *Apollo Belvedere* went on show in Julius the Second's museum. And look what a sweet and gracious work this *Pietà* is when compared with that ugly *Bacchus* that young Buonarroti carved at the same time. My poetic predecessor Shelley saw as clearly through the Neoplatonic fog as a Polish sea-eagle hunting crabs on the Mazurian lakes when he wrote that 'the countenance of this figure is the most revolting mistake.' When you read those late pious poems of Michelangelo, what do you really read? A Neoplatonist numskull fiddling with double meanings? Or a sincere, troubled religious mind trying to come to terms with the prospect of death. What possible Neoplatonic nonsense could Michelangelo have intended when he wrote the lines 'Dear God, I put myself into your hands; / Smooth the rough waves on which my ship must float. / The thorns, the nails, the wounds in both your palms, / The gentleness, the pity on your face / For great repentance, these have promised grace. / My soul will find salvation in your arms'? Zephyr! You and your neopagan kind can examine these words—'My soul will find salvation in your arms'— examine them until all the snakes in Laocoon country come home and squeeze you into milkshakes and those sacred words will not yield anything other than their obvious and true meaning. Son of Zephyr! When you look up at the Sistine ceiling and see the Almighty raise His hand to create Light and Dark, to fashion Adam with a wave of His Pentacostal finger, when you watch the Flood washing away the sins and sinners of this world—and God knows there are enough of you about—when you see all of this, it must be as clear to you as God made the Sun and the Moon that what pious Michelangelo painted on the Sistine ceiling is the Simple Religious Truth, as told in the Old Testament, as dictated to the Prophets by the Almighty Himself."

"So how do you explain all those nude boys up there?"

Derwent Blueberg had spoken in anger for the first time. He was obviously a braver man than he looked.

"I mean, I can understand Adam being short of a stitch or two, but what about all those nude guys holding up the oak leaves that are scattered all over the roof? There's nothing in the Bible, Old or New Testament, that says: And God created the heavens while a bunch of nude bodybuilders looked on getting their butts cold. I think you're oversimplifying the biblical case here, Sister."

"No, you Bluebottle or Bluestain, or whatever your silly American name is, you Blueberger are betraying your insurmountable, unacceptable, undeniable, and total religious ignorance."

"If I could just intervene here for a moment. There is a point of detail I think I can clear up." It was Professor Zephyr, staging a little resurrection of his own and entering once more into our noble discussion. "I expect you to know that the oak garlands which the geniuses are holding refer, of course, to Julius the Second. The oak was the coat of arms of the della Rovere family. If you look closely at the ceiling you'll see acorns everywhere, most prominantly, of course, above the main entrance to the chapel in the large stucco emblem surmounting the door. Now tell me, Sister Korona, you've guided a thousand tour groups through the Sistine, so which prophet do you also find painted above the door, above the della Rovere emblem?"

"Why, Zechariah, of course."

"Exactly. Zechariah. Why did Michelangelo place Zechariah above the entrance door in just about the most prominent position in the chapel when Zechariah is no more than a minor prophet? How is it that Zechariah is given this honor while Isaiah, Ezekiel, Jeremiah, who are all liturgically more important than he, are given lesser positions? I will tell you why. Because it was Zechariah who foretold that the church in Jerusalem would be rebuilt. And Zechariah also foretold who would do the rebuilding. What exactly does it say in Zechariah 6:12? It says: 'Tell him that the Lord Almighty says, "The man who is called The Branch will flourish where he is and *rebuild the Lord's Temple*."' Who is this mysterious man called 'The Branch,' who, according to Zechariah, will rebuild the Lord's Temple? I'll tell you who it is, or at least I'll tell you who thought it was he who had been named for the task. Julius the Second, of course—the della Rovere oak. That is why the della Rovere family put so much energy into rebuilding the Vatican. They believed they had been chosen. Not only did Sixtus the Fourth erect the Sistine Chapel, but Julius somehow found the nerve to knock down old St. Peter's, which had stood on its holy spot for over one thousand years. How did Julius find that nerve to start from religious and architectural scratch? How did he find the nerve to fight Bologna, Venice, the French? Why did he put so much energy into restoring the papal lands and expanding the Catholic empire in the Americas? Because he believed he had been called to do so. Because God gave him the nerve. Because The Oak thought he was The Branch. That is why he had himself painted by Raphael presiding over the renaissance of the church on the walls of his new Vatican apartments. That is why he moved out of the old apartments, which had been inhabited and decorated by the Borgia pope who had brought the church to the brink of ruin. That is why he commissioned Michelangelo to decorate the Sistine ceiling with what is essentially a tribute to the ecclesiastical new order of the della Rovere papacy."

"Let me get this clear, Zephyr. Are you saying that Julius the Second himself designed the Sistine ceiling? And that instead of seeing it as a work of individual religious genius that took Michelangelo four years hanging in the air to complete, we should actually be viewing it as a private monument to a deluded Renaissance despot who thought he had been named in the Bible?"

"Not quite, Blueberg. Not quite. That would be far too simplistic, although nearer to the truth, I venture to add, at the risk of bringing Sister Korona's wrath down upon my head once again, than the dreamy cosmic speculations of the Michelangelo-gazers."

"Professor Zephyr, there is something you have omitted to mention." Encouraged by Zephyr's perseverance in the face of so much striking enmity (Sister Korona was bubbling and steaming now like Vesuvius), I too found the courage to speak again. "When Sixtus the Fourth built the Sistine Chapel, he deliberately gave it the dimensions of Solomon's Temple in Jerusalem. Those dimensions are presented exactly in the Bible in First Kings, chapters six to fourteen. They are still the dimensions of the chapel today. So the Sistine is literally and metaphorically the Lord's new Temple as prophesied by Zechariah and rebuilt by the della Rovere Oak. Did you know that there are in fact nine species of oak in Palestine? The largest of them is *Quercus ilex,* or what we call the holm oak. Sister Korona knows, as a guide to the Vatican museums—although I believe she is very much a part-time guide . . . "

There was a whizz and a roar like a passing goose. The stone bench shuddered. Before I could finish my sentence, I was flat on my back with a pair of bony hands entwined about my throat. Laocoon himself can hardly have gasped deeper for breath than I was forced to gasp as Sister Korona's hard fingers tightened around my neck. Consonants dripping with her venom plopped into my face: "Beelzebub. Bedeviler. Beast. Bedbug." I could feel Zephyr tugging at my right arm, attempting to pull me from beneath her. "Antichrist. Archfiend. Ahriman." Blueberg was yanking at my left arm, blindly nullifying Zephyr's efforts on the other side. "Heathen. Pagan. Botanist. Oak-lover." This surely was it. The four of us were squirming around in the dust like a litter of piglets. The Lord was pronouncing me guilty of Darwinism. A blinding flash of light exploded in my eyes. Ffffuuuutttttz. The end . . .

"Excuse me, please. I forgot to wind on. Please, can you stay just like that for one moment longer. Very satisfactory. Hold it. Hold it." Ffffffuuutttz. "Very satisfactory. Thank you. Please accept my gratitude for coming so energetically to my assistance. My name is Teibi Katayama. Which one of you has captured the wagtail?"

Sister Korona had relaxed her grip enough for me to lift my head from the gravel and peep out from under her veil. Katayama was standing to attention in the middle of the courtyard, gracefully bowing, a Japanese tourist of the old school, around sixty, I would say, with a big old-fashioned Pentax slung around his neck and an even more old-fashioned English deerstalker hat pulled down over his ears so that the flaps waggled when he talked: "The wagtail entered the courtyard at seven minutes past two and thirteen seconds. It was captured at seven minutes past two and nineteen seconds. I will make a note of that."

Derwent Blueberg was the first of our party to get up off the ground and lever himself back onto the stone bench: "Er, Mr. Katayama, there's no wagtail here."

"No wagtail. Then why were you rolling around on the ground with your friends?"

Blueberg, who had just shown himself to be very slow indeed on all fours, now proved how quick he could be on his feet. "We were just horsing around. Acting something out. We were acting out David killing Goliath. When the holy sister raised her right arm as if to bring it crashing down on the young man's neck, she was imitating the upraised sword hand of the hero David as he prepares to slay the defeated giant Goliath on the walls of the Sistine Chapel."

"Aaah *so des'ka*! You were acting out the painting by Michelangelo in the Chapel of the Sistine!"

"Something like that."

Zephyr pulled himself up onto the bench, then the sister, and finally me. I dusted myself down and slumped in next to Blueberg. Nobody was saying anything except this Teibi Katayama, who was telling us his entire life story.

"That is a most pleasing coincidence. You see, it is the Chapel of the Sistine that brings me here as well. The Chapel of the Sistine and the advice of my wife, Hiroko. One morning this January my wife switched on her television in order to catch up with the state of health of our Emperor—may the sun-goddess warm his soul. It so happened that one of our main television networks, NTV, was showing a program about Rome and the restoration of the ceiling in the Chapel of the Sistine. Because of the nature of my job, Hiroko saw immediately that this program would be of interest to me. As I was already at work, she recorded the program on a videotape. You see, I am a teacher of comparative religions at Tokyo University. Perhaps you are now thinking to yourselves: Why should a godless people like the Japanese be interested in comparing other people's religions when they do not even possess a properly constructed religion of their own? But it is precisely because we do possess an improperly constructed religion that it is of such interest to us. And of course to you. I see you shaking your head from side to side in agreement, Holy Sister. No doubt you already know that this is why the wagtail is so important. When I came home that evening and saw the video of the restoration work in the Eternal City, what caught my attention was the scene in which the first man and woman are ejected from Paradise by your bearded god because the woman tempts the man with an apple from the tree of knowledge. Clearly a mythological euphemism for the discovery of sexual relations. My specialty, as the Holy Sister, who is now shaking her head most vigorously in agreement, obviously knows already, is in creation myths. Even more interesting to me than the figures of your first ancestors was the landscape in which the painter Michelangelo had placed them. If this landscape truly represented the Christian Garden of Eden, it would surely be of a more pleasing and luxuriant aspect. Why has your Michelangelo—no, why has *our* Michelangelo—constructed his paradise out of one dry tree and a handful of rocks in imitation of a Japanese Zen garden? Surely the Christian Paradise, if it really was meant to be the Christian Paradise, would contain more trees, animals, flowers, birds. . . . That was when I saw the wagtail that Michelangelo had cleverly included in his picture."

"Professor Katayama, my name is Zephyr, Edgar Zephyr, Professor Edgar Zephyr. I have made a lifelong study of Renaissance matters in general and the Sistine fresco in particular, and I can assure you that there is no wagtail on the Sistine ceiling. Indeed, the only animal

Michelangelo has included in the expulsion scene is the lower half of a snake, which he has attached to the top half of a woman to represent Satan. Unless, of course, you count the omnipresent bucranium, or ox skull, which appears at all the junctions of the illusionistic architectural surround, and which I presume alludes to Patience. That, at least, is how it is used in the *Hypnerotomachia Poliphili* of 1499. Ox skull, yes. Wagtail, no."

"Professor Zephyr, the wagtail is there. It is found in the shadows below the rock on the right of which the first man is leaning. The cleaning has made it possible to see it much more clearly. Nor is Michelangelo's wagtail a unique avifaunal presence in Renaissance art. You will remember Zygmunt Freud's essay on Leonardo da Vinci in which he discusses the presence of a symbolic vulture in Leonardo's *Holy Family with Saint Anne*."

"Professor Katayama, you must surely be aware that Freud's da Vinci essay has long since been discredited and that the whole birdy fantasy is based on the mistranslation of the Italian word for vulture. What the young Leonardo really saw in the dream which he recorded so vividly in his notebooks was not a vulture coming down onto his pram but—"

"Professor Zephyr, I am fully aware of the vulture controversy. It does not affect the existence of the wagtail up on the Sistine ceiling or indeed the existence of the wagtail in the original text in which Michelangelo must have found it. I refer, of course, to the early mythological chronicles of Japan known as the Nihongi cycle. In our creation myth, the Adam and Eve figures are called Izanagi no Mikoto and Izanami no Mikoto. Izanagi and Izanami have created the islands of Japan out of the floating oil which is roughly the equivalent of your own biblical idea of Chaos. But when it comes to creating living beings to inhabit the new land, our first ancestors were at a loss. Like your own Adam and Eve, they were completely sexually ignorant. That is when they saw the wagtail twitching its tail up and down by the side of a river. It was the wagtail that gave the first Japanese an idea of how sex might be attempted. The rest is, quite literally, history." Katayama allowed himself a hearty laugh at that, and gave Sister Korona a playful nudge in the ribs.

"What you are implying, Professor Katayama, is pornographic, and absolutely preposterous."

"Now hang on a minute, Sister Korona. Let the man have his say."

"Thank you, Professor . . . "

"Blueberg."

"Thank you for your support, Professor Bruebelg."

"Don't mention it. No, I'm fascinated by what you're saying. I'm pretty interested in comparative religions myself. And I've been to Japan. I was there with Goldblock in fifty-four. And I've just been back with Bob Rauschenhol for a show of his new goat pieces. I mean, if Goldblock hadn't been interested in the art of the American sand Indians, then we might never have seen Expressionist Abstraction, about which I've written a book. As a matter of fact, it was Bob Rauschenhol who arranged for me to be here now. You see, Bob, along with a whole bunch of concerned American artists, was getting very worried about the restoration work being done on the Sistine ceiling. There were all these horror stories coming out in the press claiming that the old Michelangelo was being destroyed and this new zitzed-up Day-Glo Michelangelo was taking the old one's place. So Rauschenhol, Warberg, and a few others sent this letter to the pope demanding that the restoration be stopped immediately. Since I have made color my specialty as a critic, they asked me to come over and see what I thought of the ceiling now that it's been cleaned."

"And what are your conclusions, Professor Bruebelg?"

"Well, I would say that as a color scheme, it has a lot going for it. It's bright. Light. It's unusual."

"Professor Bruebelg, it is much much more than that. It is a revelation. When I saw the NTV program on the cleaning of the chapel and noticed that wagtail hiding in the shadows of Paradise, I booked a seat on the next flight to Rome. Here at last was proof of a theory I had been working on for thirty years. Now Michelangelo himself was supplying me with the proof. There can no longer be any doubt—*wayfaring Japanese Shinto monks discovered Europe at least fifty years before the Portuguese missionary Francis Xavier landed in Japan.* They brought with them the Nihongi cycles, some of which Michelangelo must have seen. I came up here today because this very courtyard is the setting for an extraordinary fictitious conversation, written by another Portuguese traveler, Francisco da Holanda, which has been extremely helpful in my research. As luck would have it, just as I was climbing up the hill towards the church, what should appear on the pavement in front of me but a wagtail, a Roman wagtail, tail bobbing. It skipped straight into this court-yard. I am not a superstitious man, but of course I hurried after the unexpected sign. When I saw you, naturally I thought you too were trying to cap—"

At that very moment the little wagtail shot out from behind the laurel tree where it had been hiding from the commotion. Sister Korona bounced straight upward with a yelp. She pushed Teibi Katayama, who fell against Derwent Blueberg, who shoved me onto Professor Zephyr, who plopped off the end of the bench and returned once again to the dust from which he had so recently risen.

THE NUDES

The man who gave the official oration for the state of Florence at Michelangelo's funeral on July 14, 1564, was a typical Renaissance man, not only because he was a poet, a politician, a historian, and a critic, all at once; not only because he was a notorious sodomist who had been involved with a series of well-born boys, to whom he taught linguistics; not only because he was simultaneously the lover of a celebrated female prostitute; but also because immediately after he was imprisoned for having sex with a little girl, Benedetto Varchi was made consul of the Accademia Fiorentina, a solemn establishment post to which he was appointed with the full approval of the duke and the Florentine worthies. Varchi's busy Renaissance life is one long reminder of the different codes—sexual, social, and political—that were prevalent in Michelangelo's time. Private life and public service were considered as separate spheres of activity. (Theoretically, Jim Bakker could have become the next pope and Richard Nixon might have succeeded the Florentine envoy, Machiavelli).

An even more bizarre (by our standards) example of one of these convoluted Renaissance lives was the one led by the man appointed to organize the artistic program for Michelangelo's funeral, the great goldsmith Benvenuto Cellini. Cellini held a number of significant positions under the popes in Rome, the Medici dukes in Florence, and the king of France. He was also responsible for murdering at least three men. He was prosecuted a number of times for sodomy. He impregnated various members of his female staff. And eventually—in his sixties!—he settled down with a wife to father half a dozen legal children. It seems to me to be mere approximation to describe men like Cellini and Varchi as bisexual. They were more than that; these friends of Michelangelo were sexual adventurers in an age when the differences between the sexes were not as clearly delineated as they have since been by an increasingly puritanical social legislature. Among artists and intellectuals, at least, there appeared to be more than two genders in existence on the Renaissance earth. For alongside men and women there was a third sex: youth.

On February 27, 1556, Cellini was convicted of sodomy because "for about five years he had held as his apprentice a youth, Fernando di Giovanni de Montepulciano, with whom he had had carnal intercourse very many times and committed the crime of sodomy, sleeping in the same bed with him as though he were a wife." Yet this same Cellini would also record in his wonderful autobiography, the raciest artistic memoir of the Renaissance, that "as was natural at the age of twenty-nine I had taken as a servant a girl of exceptional beauty and grace whom I used to draw. . . . I used frequently to spend the night with her; and though I sleep lightly as ever did man upon this earth, yet after indulging sexual pleasure, my slumber is sometimes very deep and heavy." What was he dreaming about? Beautiful young girls or beautiful young boys? The two seem to have been indistinguishable (and interchangeable) to the Cellinis of the Renaissance. When the rival Florentine sculptor Bandinelli fell into an argument with Cellini over a state commission, he is reported to have screamed at this father of six to ten children: *"O sta' cheto, sodomitaccio"*—Shut up, you great sodomite.

The Renaissance difference between a male nude and a naked man is illustrated with perfect clarity in the first panel above the entrance to the Sistine Chapel. The panel records the Drunkenness of Noah. Noah, as the Book of Genesis curtly informs us, was the first man to plant a vineyard and therefore the first man to partake of one glass too many. In his case, rather unfortunately, it was the first glass he ever tried. Noah became the first man to get drunk and the first to retire to his tent to sleep it off, the first to remove all his clothes under the influence of alcohol, and the first to fall into a sound boozy sleep.

Genesis then relates how one of his sons, Ham, entered the tent, saw his father naked and mocked him. Ham went out and told his brothers, Shem and Japheth, who were the first recorded humans to feel shame at their father's nakedness. Edging backward into the tent with their eyes averted, they covered the naked Noah with a robe.

When Michelangelo began painting the Sistine ceiling in the summer of 1508, he started, not as you might have expected, with the great creation scenes at the altar end of the chapel, but with the Noah images at the entrance end, the public end: the Drunkenness of Noah was probably the first section of the world's greatest painting to be completed. As the cleaning has made very clear, the first quarter of the ceiling was the work of many hands. Michelangelo was still working with a clutch of helpers and apprentices brought from Florence, a typical enough team of interlocking Renaissance fresco makers. In the beginning, the Sistine ceiling was not the individualistic masterpiece it was to become in the Michelangelo myth. Even by the end it was never one man's work.

The story of Noah's drunkenness has been interpreted in various ways and with the usual degree of Sistine confusion. In the different attitudes of Noah's sons toward their father's nakedness, theologians have claimed to see a biblical prognosis of the split between Jews and Gentiles. More usually, Ham's mocking of his father is presented as a prefiguration of the mocking of Christ. Just as the Portuguese word for bread, *pão,* survives in modern Japanese as *pan,* so the name of *Ham* is still used in modern Polish by John Paul II and his countrymen to describe all porky moral reprobates. What is fascinating about Michelangelo's treatment of the drunkenness story is that in his scene *none* of the protagonists is wearing any clothes—the six-hundred-year-old Noah *and* the three young sons who are covering him up are all, in fact, undressed. But they are undressed in very different, very significant, ways. Old Noah is simply naked, the fat gathering in rolls around his stomach, his ancient penis flopping into wrinkles like the muzzle of a Pekingese. His three sons are muscular, upright, idealized precursors/descendants of the classic Greek hero. The sons of Noah might not be wearing any clothes, but for the purposes of this story they are not really naked at all. They are nudes. This crucial perceptual difference between being naked and being a nude informs all of the undressed figures in Michelangelo's work, most notably in the Sistine frescoes. Writing in 1905, the critic Romain Rolland looked up and saw "that ceiling built up of huge bodies, where tumultuous confusion and powerful unity combine to evoke the monstrous dream of a Hindu." How did Rolland know what Hindus dream? Unlike most of his audience, Michelangelo was not a realist. Eve is not, strictly speaking, a naked woman. Adam, the most famous of the two hundred or so nudes on the Sistine ceiling, is not, strictly speaking, a naked man.

With Michelangelo, there is no courtroom evidence of his sexuality. He was never arrested or imprisoned, as Benvenuto Cellini and Benedetto Varchi were. He left no

Celliniesque confessions behind, and his poems, passionate as they are, direct that passion toward both men and women. This poetry is so luxuriantly overgrown with Neoplatonic conceits that our own times can never know exactly how it was meant to be taken, although obviously Michelangelo's love poems were not written to be taken literally, any more than his nudes were meant to be seen as naked men.

To his beloved Tommaso de' Cavalieri he confessed, in 1532, "I burn, I consume myself, I cry. . . . Nearby you set me on fire, and parting, murder."

However, in an adjacent sonnet, this same passionate lover of young nobles imagines himself to be a piece of a lady's underwear: "Contented all day long that garment is / Which spreads itself but first clings to her breast," he wrote, before inveigling his imagination into another piece of the lady's lingerie: "And that small belt that knots so easily / Seems to declare, 'Unceasing my caresses.' / Would that my arms might join in such a passion."

In the first version of Sonnet XL (in Elizabeth Jennings's translations), Michelangelo confessed: "This is my state, *my Lord,* since I saw you; / Both bitterness and sweetness now can sway / My heart. You are the reason I am weak."

In the second version of Sonnet XL we read: "*Lady,* this is my state since I saw you; / Both bitterness and sweetness now can sway / My heart. You are the reason I am weak." "Lords" made the Laocoon lover weak, and so in the same breath did "Ladies."

Michelangelo was thus never a fully accepted and

fully committed homosexual of the modern kind. He belongs, rather, beside Donatello, Leonardo, Botticelli, and the painter nicknamed Sodoma (who decorated the walls of the papal apartments for Julius II, alongside Raphael) among those homogamous Renaissance artists about whom we have conflicting evidence of a conflicting sexuality. That he was homosexual in some form seems certain. That he was not homosexual, in the way we understand the word today, appears equally unarguable.

"And Adam was a gardener," exclaimed Shakespeare in *Henry VI,* Part II. Perhaps, but from close up he has the proportions of a Hercules and the languor of a reclining shah. Since the Almighty made the First Man in his own image, it was incumbent upon the Renaissance painter to present Adam as the perfect male specimen. Any imperfections in Adam would have implied the imperfection of God. The nudity of Adam was a symbolic nudity. It stood for divine perfection. It had to be the nudity of youth. It could not be a nakedness like Noah's. Of all the perfection-seeking Renaissance Adams, Michelangelo's, suspended in the center of the Sistine ceiling, is surely the most successful. So much so that from close up he is rather a bland figure.

"I always despised Adam," complained George Bernard Shaw of Adams in general and not Michelangelo's in particular, "because he had to be tempted by the woman, as she was by the serpent, before he could be induced to pluck the apple from the Tree of Knowledge. I should have swallowed every apple on the tree the moment the owner's back was turned." But then, Shaw was merrily human. Adam couldn't be.

Viewing the Sistine ceiling from a few inches away and viewing it from sixty feet below encourages two completely different sensations of pleasure. Up on the restorer's scaffolding the exhilaration you feel is private, inspired by detailing and specific effects, by intimate contact with greatness, by single notes. Down on the Sistine floor, you are made aware of the public grandeur of the work, its generalizations, Michelangelo's themes, his orchestration. From close up, Adam has no detailing. The precise crosshatching out of which his bodybuilder's torso—and most of this ceiling—is composed will make complete sense only from the Sistine floor. Only from the pavement will Adam be blessed with the lazy perfection that is his chief delight. Up on the scaffolding, it is the hugely imperfect Eve who is more captivating. What is interesting and imperfect about Eve is the fact that she has the body of a man.

It was usual practice in Renaissance studios to use male models to pose for all the figures in a composition, male and female. Of the scores of drawings that have survived from Michelangelo's workshop, there are hundreds of male anatomies carefully observed as they strain themselves into habitually difficult poses. Among these numerous leaners, twisters, stretchers, and benders, there are one or two Celliniesque maybes, an androgynous bottom, a kneeling youth of the third sex. But there is not a single verifiable female. The very least we can claim on the evidence of this studio output is that the ratio of males observed by Michelangelo to females must have been completely imbalanced, similar to that curious African butterfly *Papilio antimachus,* which has produced one female sighting for every thousand males.

Given Michelangelo's obsession with human anatomy, it seems improbable that he never actually saw a naked woman in his life. But he cannot have seen very many. And he does not appear to have looked too closely. The result is figures like his Sistine Eve: a man with clumsily attached breasts, a weird sexual hybrid with its waist in the wrong place and the biceps of a boxer.

If we cannot be certain that Michelangelo was homosexual, we can at least be absolutely sure that a number of his contemporaries thought he was. Michelangelo himself is one of several sources that supply the evidence. In 1533 he wrote back to Florence about a boy who wanted to become his apprentice, and in the letter Michelangelo recalls how the boy's protector had claimed "that if I were but to see him I should pursue him not only into the house, but into bed. I assure you that I'll deny myself that consolation, which I have no wish to filch from him. . . . " He was confident enough of his own celibacy in this instance to make a joke of the protector's suggestion that he would whisk the boy off to his bed as soon as he saw him.

Condivi, in his biography, makes a point of devoting a section to Michelangelo's reputation as a bedder of young boys: "He has loved the beauty of the human body, as one who best understands it: and among certain lewd men who do not know how to understand the love of Beauty unless it is lascivious and impure, there has been occasion to think and talk evil of him."

The total masculinity of the Renaissance studio, where painters and apprentices lived and slept together, inevitably resulted in the sweaty proximity of bodies. The sexual forces activated by this physical closeness must have been similar to the forces activated by the English public school system, or an army barracks. Michelangelo's small studio on the piazza before St. Peter's, in which he lived while he painted the Sistine ceiling, housed the various Florentine apprentices who had come down to help him. As a mean man, he would have lodged them in tight circumstances; a clutch of letters to various parents and guardians make clear that the father-son relationships into which Michelangelo entered with his apprentices were free of excessive formality. "Besides all my worries," he wrote back charmlessly to Florence, "I've now got this dunghill of a boy." The temptation of beautiful young boys, if such it was, was everywhere.

The Renaissance argued itself into thick theoretical knots in its attempts to claim that beauty—or, rather, Beauty, as the Neoplatonists preferred the word to be styled—could be admired without sexual desire. Beauty was a sign of God. Admiring a beautiful boy was—said the clever Neoplatonist—a way of worshiping God, who, after all, created man in his own image. We post-Freudians must surely see through this veneer of theology to the wishful thinking that lay beneath. The babble of the Renaissance, employing endless intellectual subterfuge to camouflage its true desires, is a common sound in dialogues and treatises. One of the oblique ways in which homosexuality was being discussed at the time Michelangelo was painting the Sistine ceiling was in arguments about the love of Socrates for his pupil Alcibiades. Was it pure or impure, sexual or platonic? Condivi, ever the innocent, is not suspicious of Socrates' motives; he continues his defense of his master's sexual behavior by comparing Michelangelo's apprentices to the Socratic pupils: " . . . as if Alcibiades, a most handsome young man, had not been loved most chastely by Socrates: from whose side, when he lay with him, it used to be said that he did not get up otherwise than as from the side of his father." It used to be said, elsewhere, by others, a lot, that Alcibiades got up from the bed of Socrates as from the side of a lover, not a philosophy tutor. This is implied, for instance, in Castiglione's celebrated guide to Renaissance behavior, *The Courtier,* published in 1528 but recording a conversation that took place in 1507, in which Cesare Gonzaga finds himself pondering the late-night master-pupil relationship of Socrates to Alcibiades and remarks: "Indeed it was a strange place and time—in bed and by night—to contemplate that pure beauty which Socrates is said to have loved without any improper desire." There is no reason to doubt that Michelangelo's pupils also left his bedside as they would have left their father's. His homosexuality seems to have been repressed, buried in psychological quicksand. Rather than cite the authority of Alcibiades, or Socrates, or Condivi, I would prefer to rely on the impeccable evidence of Michelangelo's paintings, drawings, and sculpture. It is a large body of work and nowhere in it does he betray the smallest sign of physical desire for a woman's body. There are hundreds of examples in which such a desire for a male body can be sensed. A good many of these examples are to be found above the spot in which the Catholic church has been selecting its new popes for 450 years, on the ceiling of the Sistine Chapel.

"I burn, I consume myself, I cry," Michelangelo writes to Tommaso de' Cavalieri, with typical sweaty intensity, nervously adding in another poem, "And if the vulgar and malignant crowd / Misunderstand the love with which we're blest, / Its worth is not affected in the least: / Our faith and honest love can still feel proud." Of course it could.

Like most other indisputably great artists, like Picasso, for instance, who was positively poisonous on the subject of rivals ("Alberto tries to make us regret the works he hasn't done," he said of Giacometti), like Leonardo, who wrote a childishly hostile treatise on the shortcomings of the Michelangelesque sculptor ("the marble dust flours him all over so he looks like a baker"), Michelangelo tolerated no competitors ("Why, my serving-maid would have written better," he replied to Leonardo's taunts). His official history (as dictated to Condivi) is littered with artistic enemies: Bramante, Raphael, and Leonardo are all variously insulted and accused. Not surprisingly, this instinctive hostility to his peers brought him recurring trouble in his daily life and earned him a reputation as a standoffish loner; according to Raphael he was "solitary like an executioner." It has been suggested by the various psychologists who have been attracted to Michelangelo's psyche like Renaissance anatomists to a beautiful cadaver that one reason why he was so obsessed with the perfect male body was because his own body seems to have been so visibly imperfect. Unlike the former male model Charlton Heston, who was large and muscular, Michelangelo was small and squat. According to our attracted psychologists, he probably felt particularly sensitive about his face, notably about his grotesquely broken nose. The weird self-portrait included in the cascade of pessimism on the altar wall of the Sistine Chapel, the Last Judgement, in which Michelangelo portrays himself as the unwanted skin of St. Bartholomew hanging from the saint's fist like a snake's discarded scales, obviously has specifically theological significance as a symbol of regeneration and the rebirth of the soul. But the image also carries a considerable psychological charge as evidence of a man's savage displeasure with his existing state.

The circumstances in which Michelangelo's nose was broken are entertainingly recorded by Benvenuto Cellini, who names the perpetrator. It was Piero Torrigiani, a fellow sculptor from Florence who went to work for the English monarchy and who produced the tombs of Henry VII and Elizabeth of York in Westminster Abbey. Torrigiani came back to Florence to escape from "the English beasts" who had employed him in London and to find assistants to help him embark upon another ambitious project, the tomb of Henry VIII. Cellini recorded Torrigiani's reminiscences of the good old days in Florence: "This Buonarroti and I used, when we were boys, to go into the Church of the Carmine, to learn drawing from the chapel of Masaccio. It was Buonarroti's habit to banter all who were drawing there; and one day, among others, when he was annoying me, I got more angry than usual, and clenching my fist, gave him such a blow on the nose, that I felt bone and cartilage go down like biscuit beneath my knuckles; and this mark of mine he will carry with him to the grave." Nothing in the later behavior of Buonarroti refutes Torrigiani's claim that the young sculptor had taunted and angered his fellow pupils with displays of his own superiority. Unlike Michelangelo, we should perhaps be secretly grateful to Torrigiani for leaving an indelible mark on the face of the Renaissance because that broken nose has proved an invaluable aid to identifying the various hidden self-portraits that Michelangelo produced.

Michelangelo might not have found many nude women to draw in his studio but he must surely have cut some open on the dissecting table. For he was an experienced anatomist and during at least two periods in his life he immersed himself in very detailed anatomical studies. The first was in Florence in the 1490s, before he came to Rome, when the prior of Santo Spirito allowed him access to the corpses collected in the hospital morgue. "Nothing could have given him more pleasure," Condivi writes. Michelangelo is said to have thanked the prior for this opportunity to cut up lepers and vagabonds by carving a wooden crucifix for him. This crucifix has disappeared. The rather unlikely example of painted poplar that has since surfaced in the corridor of Santo Spirito and now stands in Michelangelo's family home in Florence is definitely not the work of an anatomist.

The second opportunity to dissect bodies in numbers was in Rome in the 1540s, when Michelangelo and the surgeon Realdus Columbus devoted themselves to methodical dismemberment while preparing a new anatomical treatise, in which Michelangelo's views on the proportions of the human figure were to be collected and published. Without such anatomical study, claimed Leonardo, an equally enthusiastic dissector of corpses, the human body will look like "a sack of nuts" and the muscles of a man will resemble "a bundle of radishes." There is nothing in Michelangelo's oeuvre to compare with Leonardo da Vinci's full-frontal examinations of female sexual organs, Renaissance beaver shots that probe the human biology like a surgeon's scalpel. Michelangelo seems to have been more interested in finding out how bones and muscles define harmonious proportion than in identifying and labeling the software of the lower abdomen (which fascinated Leonardo). We know, for instance, that Michelangelo considered a knowledge of anatomy essential to the practice of architecture. Francisco da Holanda, in one of his imaginary conversations with Michelangelo, reports that the best kind of cadaver is "very lean and proportional" and describes how the skin must be removed in the Michelangelo fashion, little by little. Da Holanda's Michelangelo took the muscles out of the lean bodies and then made plaster casts of them. These could later be rearranged into working models from which movement could be studied.

Condivi also remembers an anatomy lesson Michelangelo gave him. It took place over a corpse of "a beautiful young Moor" that Colombus had supplied. Well-proportioned, lean, beautiful corpses supplied the anatomical knowledge that went into the painting of the most influential nudes on the Sistine ceiling—the twenty *ignudi* who surround the Genesis scenes and who hold up garlands of the della Rovere acorns (in case we have forgotten who commissioned this ceiling). Lean, beautiful corpses were the most exact template available of the form of Adam, and therefore of the Almighty's own likeness. It was the desire to examine how man was the measure of all things rather than some complicated psychological need to poke about in the darker stretches of science (of the kind that drove Leonardo) that motivated Michelangelo. The projected anatomical treatise was never published. According to Condivi, "Michelangelo gave up dissecting corpses. This was because his long familiarity with the practice had so upset his stomach that he could neither eat nor drink beneficially."

On a cold February morning halfway through the Sistine restoration, I found myself up on the scaffolding staring at Michelangelo's muscular Adam and his equally muscular Eve. Our First Ancestors had just been cleaned, and it was more obvious than ever that Adam's little penis was a cipher of masculinity, not a sexual organ, and that

Eve's golf-ball breasts belonged on a driving range, not on a real woman's chest. But the ability to distinguish between symbolic nudity and depraved nakedness is not one of the Catholic church's traditional strengths.

That particular morning, the plans for the cleaning of the Last Judgement, which was to follow the restoration of the Sistine ceiling, had not yet been announced. It was not yet clear what the official Vatican policy would be when work finally began on the Last Judgement below. Would the restorers remove the loincloths and other pieces of modesty-endowing drapery added to the lower regions of the naked and the damned after Michelangelo's death by his friend Daniele da Volterra—who thus has the misfortune of going down in art history by the nickname of "the breeches-painter"?

The Last Judgement is the greatest gathering of nudes in Renaissance art. All manner of bodies, guilty or not guilty, tumble through the last act of the human tragedy like washing in a spin-drier. What offended Michelangelo's contemporaries most profoundly seems not to have been the wholesale nudity of his damned souls—the *ignudi* on the ceiling are just as naked as the damned in the Last Judgement, yet no pope ever seriously suggested they be girded—but the fresco's overt message that, come the Last Judgement, all will stand equal before their Maker, men, women, saints, sinners, Vatican officials, and popes. That was Lutheran talk. Michelangelo had turned the Sistine Chapel into what Adrian VI, a Dutchman choking on his own piety, the last non-Italian pope before John Paul II, had described as a *stufa,* or brothel.

Michelangelo was, wrote one observer to Florence, "the inventor of filth." The creepy Aretino, who has been described as the first "journalist" of his century, wrote an open letter to Michelangelo that did more than any other single document to whip up the zealots who wanted the Last Judgement condemned. Slyly he suggested that Michelangelo was a homosexual. "Such things might be painted in a voluptuous bathroom, but not in the choir of the highest chapel," he spat.

Even though the cleaning of the Sistine ceiling has exposed with new vividness just how extensive and sensuous a celebration of male nudity the fresco is, there is once again an awkward and unworthy silence at the Vatican on the subject of Michelangelo's homosexuality. It needs saying very loudly indeed that had he not been a homosexual of the Renaissance kind he could never have painted the greatest masterpiece of Christian art.

In the church of S. Maria sopra Minerva, in the heart of Michelangelo's old Rome, at the foot of the altar, is a white marble statue, Michelangelo's *Resurrected Christ,* bearing the cross and a palm pole, symbols of his passion. According to an ingenious theory outlined by the provocative Michelangelo scholar David Summers, this resurrected Christ is a kind of template for the well-proportioned human being. The palm pole he holds is marked off at regular intervals into segments that divide the body into its optimum anatomical lengths. Had Michelangelo's anatomical treatise been published, this might have been his model of the perfect man. Be that as it may, what is certain is that Michelangelo's *Risen Christ,* like the parallel

Christ figure in the Last Judgement, was originally as naked as the Bible ordains he should be: when the Apostles entered the tomb after the crucifixion, Jesus was not there and they, "looking in, saw the linen clothes lying." John's Gospel, 20:5, makes it plain—Christ was resurrected as he was born on this earth, completely naked.

Disregarding this clear biblical advice, the church authorities at S. Maria sopra Minerva decided some centuries ago that their faithful needed to be protected from the sight of Christ's nakedness. A clumsy metal loincloth was fashioned and stuck onto the statue. During the pontificate of the liberal Pope John XXIII, this metal loincloth was removed, and Michelangelo's quiet *Risen Christ* was once again completely nude, as the artist intended him to be, as St. John explicitly says he ought to be. Now this ugly bit of false drapery has been put back.

THE GOLD

Now, Michelangelo was superstitious. Otherwise how could Condivi have known that on the night that Michelangelo was born in the year of our Savior 1475, the sixth day of March, four hours before daybreak, on a Monday, at that exact moment Mercury with Venus had propitiously entered the house of Jupiter, and both were peaceably disposed. This promised a splendid future for Lodovico di Lionardo Buonarroti Simoni's new son: the offspring would be of such noble and lofty talent as to triumph in all and every enterprise, but principally, as Condivi appends, in those arts that delight the senses. He meant painting, sculpture, architecture. Condivi could have known Michelangelo's horoscope only if Michelangelo had given it to him.

WITH MORE
APOLOGIES TO
FRANCISCO DA
HOLANDA

Sister Korona was also superstitious—as the pious and the Polish frequently become—and she had ducats on her mind, thousands and thousands of ducats. As she slumbered in the shade of the laurel tree in the courtyard of S. Silvestro, her sharp chin embedded in the snowy white chest of her habit like an icepick, thousands of Sistine ducats tumbled through her imagination in cascades of gold, while the voice of the intoning Derwent Blueberg lullabied her ever more deeply into dreaminess. Blueberg had that morning purchased from a Roman antique dealer a gold coin which he believed to be a genuine Giulian ducat minted at the time of Michelangelo's Sistine campaign. He had passed the coin around for our inspection ("an obvious forgery," said Zephyr) and was now lecturing the assembled on the subject of dosh, shekels, filthy lucre, readies, notes to you and me, greenbacks, or, in this case, goldbacks, the papal payment to Michelangelo: "It seems he was paid only three thousand ducats for his work on the Sistine ceiling. Tolgate says it was six thousand ducats. But his evidence flops. It was three thousand ducats."

Sister Korona, had she been awake, could have supplied Derwent Blueberg with some evidence, the evidence of numbers and the divine intrusion in digits, the supreme evidence of total numismatic coincidence. Because three thousand ducats was the exact sum that Shylock, the Jew, loans to Antonio, the Gentile, in Shakespeare's *Merchant of Venice,* with a pound of Antonio's flesh offered as fifteen hundred years of biblical security in return. This Shylock, according to Sister Korona's hair-trigger imagination,

cackled like Booz addressing his Fool's stick when Antonio
was late with his repayment: "You'll ask me why I rather
choose to have / A weight of carrion flesh than to receive/
Three thousand ducats. I'll never answer that; / But say
it is my humour." Humorous ducats by the bucket, thirty
pieces of silver turned into gold and multiplied by ten
and ten again, by the sins of man and the critical number
of the cosmos: Odysseus wandered for nine years and
returned on the tenth; and they called Michelangelo the
Homer of Painting. Ten times thirty times ten. Sister
Korona's chin pings out and upward, her eyes strain to
open, she wants so much to tell the assembled of her
discovery, but her rambling consciousness is not yet ready
to return, and the icepick chin plunges down once more,
anchoring the dreams of Sister Wiktorja Korona in the
region of her heart.

"As we already know, Shakespeare was born in the
year Michelangelo died. 'Hath a dog money?' splutters
Shylock in *The Merchant of Venice*. 'Is it possible / A cur
can lend three thousand ducats?' Yes he can," continued
Blueberg, "he can lend it to Antonio. And if we swap the
name Bramante for the insulted 'cur,' then our rhetorical
questioner can lend the three thousand ducats to Raphael.
Raphael needs them to buy a new house."

I must admit that none of this was making any sense
to me at all. But then I was wide awake and listening,
squeezed onto the stone bench between Blueberg and
Zephyr, trying to elbow out some thinking room. Clearly
you had to be fast asleep and dreaming like Sister Korona
leaning Pisa-tower-style against Teibi Katayama for Der-

went Blueberg's lofty fiscal speculations to come into true focus. The sleeping Sister Korona was following his arguments perfectly. Indeed, she was way ahead of him. What she possessed, and I did not, was the information divulged that very morning to thirty-four Polish seminarians from Lodz, in Bernini's piazza, in midtour: that when Raphael of Urbino settled down in Rome as Michelangelo's chief rival, he bought a house in the Borgo from Michelangelo's other great artistic enemy, Bramante. The palace—indeed the entire neighborhood—was later flattened by the Fascists when they rationalized the approaches to the Vatican. Sister Korona knew how much Raphael had paid Bramante for his house. Three thousand ducats, of course. She was dying to wake up and beat Blueberg to the announcement of this figure, but her stubborn Polish eyes would not open. So Blueberg told us the price of Raphael's palace and continued his trudge through a chaotic numismatic history, uninterrupted:

"The ducat was first struck by Roger the Second of Sicily and bore the inscription '*Sit tibi, Christe, datus, quem tu regis, iste ducatus*'—Lord, thou rulest this duchy, to thee be it dedicated. That is how the coin came to be called the ducat, a ducal object of dedication. It was certainly not, as Tolgate claims, because the duchy of Venice also struck such a gold coin in the thirteenth century. When Hamlet shouts: 'Dead, for a ducat, dead!' he is hardly likely to have been aware that three thousand ducats was how much Michelangelo was promised for painting the Battle of Cascina in the council hall in Florence, the commission that so impressed Julius the Second that he called Michelangelo to Rome. It is my belief that the naked figures of soldiers bathing before the battle correspond in obvious ways to the figures of the damned in the Flood up on the Sistine roof. In the Battle of Cascina you see three thousand gold ducats' worth of Florentine soldiers caught with their trousers down, literally, by the attacking Pisans. In the Flood you see the early humans sinning in the rain, ark-less. Retribution sneaks up on all of them. Even more significant than that, as far as my thesis is concerned, is the fact that the marbles acquired from Carrara by Michelangelo for Julius's tomb cost—you guessed it—three thousand ducats!"

"What exactly is your thesis, Professor Blueberg?" Edgar Zephyr interjected, finally giving verbal form to a question that had been scampering around all our thoughts for some minutes.

"My thesis? My thesis is no longer a thesis as such. My thesis is better than a thesis. It is a factoid. There are three hundred figures on the Sistine ceiling. And ten bronze medallions representing the sins of man, and of course the Commandments given to Moses and counted out in Deuteronomy. If you multiply the number of figures by the sins of man, you get the number of ducats Michelangelo was paid to paint the ceiling. You also get the number of ducats he received for painting the Sala del Consilio, the number of ducats he paid for the marbles of the Julius tomb, the price of the house Raphael bought from Bramante, and the exact loan given to Antonio by Shakespeare's Merchant of Venice—a fact that only gains its true cosmic significance when you remember that

Shakespeare was born in the year Michelangelo died. What I haven't told you yet is that Michelangelo's exact contemporary, Copernicus, Sister Korona's countryman, was then in Rome expounding his theory that the earth revolves around the sun and that up on the Sistine ceiling the sun and the moon . . ."

At the mention of Copernicus, Sister Korona was finally inspired to poke her head up through the elasticated envelope of sleep. She rose out of her slumbers with her eyes closed, like the shark in *Jaws*: "Blueberg. You have stolen my speculation. You have inveigled my dreams. Burgled my subconscious. I was dreaming myself to exactly the same conclusion. The three thousand ducats were divinely ordained, were they not?" She never heard the answer, for no sooner was the question asked than the elastic of sleep contracted again, and the sweet afternoon bath of the siesta tugged Sister Wiktorja Korona back into its warm psychological waters. But she had made her point. The ability of the truly religious to be truly superstitious at the same time never ceases to amaze me.

We were five again, gathered in the courtyard of S. Silvestro under the laurel tree, called hither to present our conclusions on the meaning of the Sistine ceiling. Wishing to understand the ceiling was the terrible vice we all shared. Every one of us had made a pact with the same Sistine devil: Curiosity. Katayama had already spoken, briefly, informing us that he had acquired definite proof of the nonexistence of the Nihongi wagtail. Blueberg had spoken on the subject of gold. Korona had spoken of divine digital determination—albeit in her sleep. Soon it would be my turn. But in this courtyard, age had been preceding beauty for five hundred years, ever since Francisco da Holanda allowed the fictitious Vittoria Colonna to be overtured by the counterfeit Michelangelo in that fraudulent dialogue of his. Zephyr got in before me.

"Professor Blueberg's oration on the color of money, horribly misleading though it was, introduced us, by complete accident, to the central mystery of the Sistine ceiling: the Janus effect. Let me ask you all a riddle. What is golden, has two sides, and makes the world go round?"

"The ducat," said Blueberg.

"The yen," said Katayama.

"Zlotys," muttered Sister Korona in her sleep.

"The sun," said I, beating Zephyr at his own game. It was a trick he had tried to pull in his book *Mysterious Pagans of the Renaissance,* in a discussion of the Apollo cult. It so happened that my own Sistine thesis revolved, like Copernicus's earth, around the sun painted by Michelangelo in the most prominent position on the Sistine ceiling. In the sooty gloom of the old chapel, we had tended naturally to assume that the creation of Adam was the aerial focus of the fresco. Those nearly touching fingers had been hogging not only the Sistine's iconographic limelight but also whatever real light managed to penetrate the papal brazier fumes. But the cleaning had revealed the ceiling's true epicenter. It had finally confirmed Michelangelo's pellucid intentions. He had wanted the eye of the congregation to be drawn first not to the manufacture of Man Number One but to the brightest object on the Sistine roof, the fiery ball of gold created by the Almighty on the third day of Genesis, the sun, the origin of all life, a symbol for the divine energy of the Godhead itself. I believed that Michelangelo's color symbolism had been obscured by five hundred years of papally induced darkness. When the brightest object on the ceiling was turned by soot into a squidge of gray, the Sistine ceiling lost not only its sunshine but also its sense. Just to rub it in I repeated my answer. "The solution to your riddle, Professor Zephyr, is: the sun. The sun is golden. It has two sides, the day and the night. And at exactly the moment Michelangelo was painting the Sistine ceiling Copernicus was imagining how the earth went around the sun, and not vice versa."

"Wrong. The answer to my riddle is *free will*. Free will is the Almighty's most precious gift to mankind. Michelangelo's favorite writer, Dante, terms it thus in the *Divine Comedy*: 'The greatest gift that God in His bounty made in creation and that which he prizes the most, was the freedom of will, with which the creatures with intelligence, they all and they alone, were and are endowed.' Free will, like Blueberg's ducats, has two sides, a heads and a tails—"

"My ducats!? Now just hang on a minute, Zephyr. The ducats belong in the intellectual arena along with—"

"—to sin or not to sin, to seek salvation or damnation, that is the question that Michelangelo's God asks, to be echoed by Blueberg's Shakespeare—."

"My Shakespeare!? You are out of order here, professor—"

"— free will makes the world go round because, as Machiavelli writes in *The Prince,* 'God is not willing to do everything, and thus take away our free will and that share of glory that belongs to us."

"That's all very nice and biblical, Zephyr, but what in Zerubbabel's name does it have to do with the iconographic stasis of the Sistine ceiling?"

"Everything, Blueberg. Everything. I draw your attention to the second panel of Genesis that Michelangelo has arranged above the altar. You will recall that it contains two portraits of the Supreme Being, two Almightys in one picture, a front view and a back view, a heads and a tails. One Supreme Being is flying towards the congregation, having created the sun, and the other is flying away, having finished the earth. It's a sort of Renaissance split-screen effect. And it completely bamboozled Michelangelo's first biographer, Paulo Giovio, Bishop of Nocera, who, you may remember, was so confused by this divine to-ing and fro-ing that he did not even recognize his Creator. In Giovio's thirty-one-line biography of Michelangelo, God—both Gods, if you like—is, or are, curtly described as 'an old man flying through the air.' Various commentators have tried to admire this extraordinary two-pronged Almighty for His, or Their, formal accomplishment by assuming that Michelangelo is merely showing off his prowess as a foreshortener, perhaps the finest foreshortener that ever lived. But for a man of Michelangelo's enormous biblical integrity, the need for a display of artistic prowess would never have been reason enough to cut Jehovah in half, to duplicate the Divine Being. No. The Neoplatonic core of his symbolism is surely obvious enough: the Godhead has a heads and a tails. The Creator gives and He takes away. For every birth there is a death. As Donne put it in his epitaph: "the furthest East and the furthest West . . . so death doth touch the resurrection." One godly pronouncement begins life on earth; the other ends it. The same God who created the day also created the night. That surely is the meaning of the subsequent scenes that Michelangelo has arranged along the Sistine vault. At every step they echo the essentially dualistic nature of our existence. Man, having been endowed with free will, makes his choices— and up there on the Sistine ceiling he pays his dues. Man is as noble as his Maker. But he is also as low as the lowest life form defecating in the woodwork of Noah's storm-tossed ark. Man demands salvation. The Christian church offers it to him. Blueberg, you claim to be an expert on Shakespeare—"

"I made no such claim, I merely posited—"

"— and, as an expert on Shakespeare, you of all men must know what it was that the first clown in *Hamlet* said about the First Man, Act Five, Scene One. The first clown said: 'There is no ancient gentleman but gardeners, ditchers, and gravemakers; they hold up. . . .' What, Blueberg, what? What is it that your Shakespeare gives these ancient grave-diggers to uphold? Since you do not answer me, I will answer you. They uphold, according to the first clown, 'Adam's profession.' You may have forgotten your high-school Shakespeare, Blueberg, but you have already proved to us, at considerable length, that you have not forgotten how to count up to three thousand. You will therefore know exactly how many of these Adams are to be found on the Sistine ceiling?" At that precise moment Derwent Blueberg's Adam-counting faculties went down like a disconnected computer. "There are four Adams on the Sistine ceiling, Blueberg. Four First Men. One is being created by the Almighty in the famous display of finger-touching that Professor Katayama has emblazoned across his chest. A splendid T-shirt, Professor Katayama. So youthful. The next Adam is sleeping while Eve emerges from his prostrate body. Finally, at the heart of the fresco, two more First Men are being tempted by a pair of First Women. One of these Adams still resides in the Garden of Eden. The other has succumbed to Eve's embraces—and is being expelled from Paradise. How did Samuel Butler put it in *Hudibras*? 'The extremes of glory and of shame / Like east and west become the same.' As we look down the Sistine vault from the congregation's point of view, towards the altar, this essential human duality is stressed at every painterly step. The right side of the ceiling is devoted to the east of the human condition—if I may call it that—and the left to the human west. On the right, man makes the correct choices and on the left, he sins. How many Noahs are there in the scene of his drunkenness, Blueberg?"

"Two," croaked the chief apologist of Expressionist Abstraction, a beaten man, seriously in need of a stiffener himself.

"Exactly. Two Noahs. One on the right who is fully clothed and who toils industriously in the field. And one on the left who is naked, for he has chosen the path of self-degradation and lies in a drunken stupor in his tent. On the left-hand side of the Flood, the Sistine congregation sees a mountaintop crowded with damned souls about to be swallowed by the divine torrent. On the right they see Noah's ark, a floating temple representing the Christian church, salvation, the rising sun, the true path, the east of hu—"

"Actually, Professor Zephyr, there are five Adams on the ceiling in the Chapel of the Sistine. Not four. You are wrong."

Teibi Katayama had not said much that day. Earlier in the afternoon, he had quietly described a traumatic visit to the Sistine restoration.

Since our last meeting Teibi had acquired a zoom lens and gone properly armed into the chapel to photograph the Nihongi wagtail, only to find that the use of a flash was not permitted. Frightening his way past the guard on the elevator by pretending to be the Japanese film actor Toshiro Mifune, Teibi had scaled the scaffold and positioned himself beneath the First (or second in the sequence) Man; he had peered deep into the newly cleaned darkness beneath Adam's arm: no wagtail. The chief restorer confidently confirmed its lack of presence, a trick of the light, a smudge of candle soot. This news had saddened our jovial company and induced a communal nervousness. All of us shared Katayama's wicked addiction to the Sistine truth.

"The fifth Adam you have forgotten to include in your interesting thesis," he now continued, visibly perking up, "is the old Adam who is seen officiating at the sacrifice being offered to your Lord by the first man's first sons, Cain and Abel. All the choices between the good path and the bad path that you describe, Professor Zephyr, are exemplified in the tale of the first man's offspring. When Abel chooses to sacrifice his first lamb, he is selecting the correct path. When Cain chooses merely to sacrifice a little of his harvest, he is selecting the incorrect path, the path of selfishness. His sacrifice is not enough of a sacrifice. When Cain then murders Abel because Abel had made a better sacrifice than he has, Cain is confirming his incorrect choice and echoing the dilemma of his father, the first man."

"Professor Katayama, I do not wish to contradict you, but the scene you refer to, which I believe is the seventh scene along if you start from the Creation, that scene does not show the sacrifice of Cain and Abel. The young men in the picture are not Cain and Abel. They are the sons of Noah dividing up the animals into clean and unclean ones, kosher and not kosher, as Blueberg might say, those you should sacrifice and those you should not, backing up my central thesis about the duality of the human condition. Western scholarly opinion is united in believing that this seventh scene, in fact, represents the Sacrifice of Noah, who is shown thanking the Lord for granting him salvation from the Great Flood."

"Professor Zephyr, Western scholarly opinion has clearly made a mistake. Condivi states quite categorically that the scene represents Cain and Abel. And there really is no reason not to believe him, other than the vanity of twentieth-century scholarship. The sacrifice of Cain and Abel is chronologically correct, whereas the sacrifice of Noah took place after the great flood, not, as it is shown here, before it. Are you seriously suggesting that Michelangelo tinkered with the chronology of your Bible when he had no need to?"

"Professor Katayama, you are looking at the ceiling the wrong way. That is why you are having this little Oriental difficulty in understanding it. The correct way to imagine those nine central panels is not sequentially, as nine pictures in a row. You have to see them—as I believe Julius Klaczko first pointed out—as three sets of triptychs. The Sacrifice of Noah does not precede the Flood—it flanks the Flood, with the Drunkenness of Noah on the other side."

"Professor Zephyr, I am intrigued by your suggestion that Michelangelo was working chronologically for two-thirds of his triptych of triptychs and then decided to spend the third triptych not being chronological after all. How very Western of him."

"Professor Katayama, there are no figures in the scene you mention that can be identified with Cain and Abel."

"Professor Zephyr, there are two very obvious figures in the scene to be identified with Cain and Abel. The young man who cuts the ram's throat and who offers up the rather unpleasant bundle of blood to the priestess is evidently Abel."

An offering of blood. So that was what the priestess

is receiving. This mysterious red blob had been puzzling Michelangelo-watchers for 450 years. It had grown so much brighter since the cleaning. I was beginning to warm to Katayama's sensible Eastern ideas.

"Do not forget," he continued, "that the blood which Abel is offering up for sacrifice is not just the sheep's. It is his own blood as well, for he is about to die at the hands of Cain. So Abel is what you yourself, Professor Zephyr, might term a proto-Christ. Abel is about to make the ultimate sacrifice. The young man on the right who carries a bundle of sticks for the fire is therefore Cain. If you count the sticks, you will see there are seven. When Cain murders Abel and your Lord expels Cain and Cain replies to the Lord that everyone will try to kill a homeless wanderer, your Lord is quoted in your Bible telling your ancestor Cain: 'If anyone kills you, seven lives will be taken in revenge.' Seven sticks for seven deaths. 'So the Lord put a mark on Cain to warn anyone who met him not to kill him.' "

"'And Cain went from the Lord's presence and lived in a land called 'Wandering,' which is east of Eden.' Dean's finest performance, don't you think?" continued Blueberg. We ignored him.

"Professor Katayama, you have misplaced the essential problem. The Bible says quite clearly that Adam and Eve had only two sons, the good Abel and the bad Cain. Yet in the scene you mention, there are four sons attending the sacrifice. Two attending to the sheep. Two attending to the fire."

"Professor Zephyr, you yourself have already pointed

out that there are two Adams in one scene and two Noahs and two Almightys in another. Clearly Michelangelo was not an orthodox counter of biblical figures. What we have here is two Abels and two Cains. One Abel brings the good sheep; the other cuts its throat. One Cain carries the seven sticks of guilt; the other Cain throws them on the fire and stares deep into the flames of eternal damnation—his future. If you are taking the biblical text literally, Professor Zephyr, then your Almighty, unlike Professor Bruebelg here, cannot count. If Cain and Abel are Adam and Eve's only offspring, then the Almighty does not have to put a mark on Cain, as there would be no one else already in existence to murder him. And where on earth would the Almighty find the seven lives to take in revenge if Cain was killed? If the scene does represent the sons of Noah, why are there four boys and not three? Noah's sons, you will remember, were Shem, Ham, and Japheth. What did your Almighty say to your Cain? He said: 'Because you have done evil, sin is crouching at your door.' What has Michelangelo painted behind Cain? A black doorway, Professor Zephyr. A black doorway."

"Professor Katayama, I admire your reasoning, but I can assure you that several generations of Christian scholars have been in complete agreement that the scene you describe is the Sacrifice of Noah and that Noah himself is the old man officiating at the sacrifice."

"Professor Zephyr, I can assure you that the old man is Adam. Otherwise how can you explain the two female figures who flank him at the altar? One is a young priestess representing Virtue, the other is Eve in old age, still whispering temptation in his ear, and still therefore representing Vice. Old Adam is shown in the standard Renaissance dilemma known as the choice of Hercules, having to choose between vice and virtue."

"Professor Katayama. It's the Sacrifice of Noah."

"Professor Zephyr. The old man is Adam."

"Noah."

"Adam."

"I said Noah."

"And I said Adam."

"NOAH!!!"

"ADAM!!!!"

"Gentlemen, gentlemen, please. Let us maintain some scholarly decorum here. There's only one way to sort this out. Heads is Noah. Tails is Adam. We'll toss for it." And with that, Derwent Blueberg gave his newly purchased gold ducat a mighty twist and flick. It soared through the air in a sweet arc and landed cleanly in the dark chasm of Sister Korona's snoring mouth. Thence it disappeared from sight immediately, like Jonah swallowed by the whale.

THE EQUIPMENT

When Rome falls, warned Byron in *Childe Harold's Pilgrimage,* the World falls. Which could be why so much frantic energy went into keeping the place standing during the 1980s. In St. Peter in Chains, Michelangelo's famously stern *Moses* sat squeezed between the old church of stone and a new inner church of plastic sheeting, like a fly trapped in the double-glazing. If you looked down on the Foro Romano from the delightful Piazza del Campidoglio, which Michelangelo designed on the Capitoline Hill, you witnessed the grand surrealism of chronically ruined arches and colonnades being turned into odd-shaped blue plastic parcels as ruin after ruin was comprehensively modernized. Those matching antique phalluses that have been drawing visitors to Rome for fifteen

hundred years, the columns of Trajan and Marcus Aurelius, were both under wraps and stood there in their
respective urban clearings looking like two lingam jokes
by Christo, the conceptual wrapper. In the middle of the
Piazza del Campidoglio itself, the equestrian statue of
Marcus Aurelius, around which Michelangelo planned this
entire architectural space, disappeared forever, leaving
only a ghostly plinth—designed by Michelangelo and
suitably antique in style. There is no more disheartening
experience lying in wait for the enthusiastic grand tourist
than the sight of a site under scaffolding. And the 1980s
Romans developed this particular department of torture
into an art form. The Pantheon became a Plankanon. S.
Maria del Popolo, the gorgeous della Rovere church,
looked from the outside like a Brazilian shanty town.

If one of those proverbial visitors from Mars happened across this melange of planks, parts, struts, sheets,
joints, joists, nuts, knots, and bolts, he, she, or it would
be forgiven for assuming that here was a city on the verge
of a complete urban collapse. But this was not the case.
The Eternal City was, in fact, a great deal more solid in
the 1980s than it has been on numerous occasions in its
interestingly riotous past. Modern English visitors were
not greeted by the appalling sights that met one of their
numbers in the mid-fifteenth century: cows grazing on
the altars of roofless churches and wolves fighting with
dogs beneath the walls of old St. Peter's. "O God,"
pleaded our mid-fifteenth-century Englishman, "how piti-
able is Rome." In today's St. Peter's it is unlikely that

the congregation will experience what it experienced on that stormy day in 1605 when a large chunk of the heavenly vault crashed down to earth in the middle of mass. Karol Wojtyla is unlikely to enter St. Peter's and be greeted by slabs of descending masonry, which is what happened to Alexander VI. The ubiquitous Roman art restorations may have created the illusion of a dilapidated city on the verge of ruin, but it is important to recognize these restorations for what they are: signs of prosperity, not of poverty; mementos of success, not of decay.

A few months after the terrible earthquake of September, 1985, that shook Mexico as violently as a dog shaking water off its back, I visited Mexico City. It is peculiarly unfortunate that in a country prone to having its walls shaken by terrible earthquakes, the painted wall has evolved into a national art form, celebrated and explored since Aztec times. The example of the pre-Hispanic mural schemes inspired Diego Rivera and the Mexican muralists to cover the walls of their capital with the greatest fresco cycles of the twentieth century. How vulnerable they are.

That vicious earthquake telescoped multistory office blocks into bungalows and turned the foyers of famous hotels into dripping caves that needed to be explored with a torch. I tiptoed unchallenged into the Ministry of Education, where Rivera's most successful and most gorgeously colored scheme was painted in a *buon fresco* technique that would have delighted Signor Colalucci and his fellow Vatican restorers. Some of the cracks that plunged through the paint surface were nine inches wide. The floors of the Ministry of Education undulated like a roller-coaster track.

The total area of these spectacular Rivera murals, arranged on all four sides and all three levels of the ministry's central cloisters, completely dwarfs Michelangelo's contribution to the Sistine ceiling. Sitting on a plank on a simple scaffold on the ground floor, having just begun repairing the terrible damage to the most accomplished frescoes of the twentieth century, was an old man in a white coat. In his left hand he had a palette, in his right a tiny brush, with which he dabbed away at the widest crack. When the Arno breached its banks in 1966, art volunteers from across the world converged on Florence in their thousands. In Mexico after the earthquake, this old man toiled alone.

This, then, is one kind of modern restoration. Let us call it "true restoration" to differentiate it from what has been taking place all around Italy in the past twenty years. True restoration is embarked upon in a hurry when serious damage has been done to a work of art. Its ambition is to make good the damage and to return the work of art to something resembling its original form. The Roman-style restoration of the Sistine ceiling we should call something else.

Up on the Sistine scaffold they had enough equipment bleeping and buzzing day and night to run an air-traffic control tower. They had an Apollo DN 3000 workstation with Italcad software and a Calcomp plotter. The restorers used the computer to digitize images from the ceiling and store them in the graphics database along with every conceivable and measurable detail of the painting's state. They could (almost) plot every brushstroke Michelangelo made on his epic journey across the vault. They could digitize the cracks and discolorations with their photographic measurement system. In the Vatican laboratories—carefully filmed in high-definition video by the Japanese makers of the NTV special—they used spectrum technology to determine the exact chemical composition of Michelangelo's pigments. The Vatican scientists easily identified the materials added in previous restorations. They easily isolated the true Michelangelo. Every day's work was logged and recorded. While the computer glowed and bleeped, digesting all the available information about the ceiling's progress, other pieces of modern art-machinery were busily recording the microclimate in the chapel itself. Hazardous changes in the Sistine atmosphere had been caused not just by the smoking candles and incense burners but even by the polluting breath of five centuries of visitors. The results of these tests encouraged a decision to install central heating to ensure the total control of the Sistine's internal weather conditions. The microprocessing of Michelangelo was the ultimate example of eighties-style computer-aided superrestoration.

True restoration seeks merely to return a work of art to some semblance of working order. Cosmetic restoration—of which the Sistine campaign was the most spectacular example—begins with a work of art that is already in working order, and extrapolates from there. Cosmetic restoration is embarked upon at a city's leisure when the historical fancy takes it. And the changes wrought by it are far more radical than those encouraged by true restoration. Cosmetic restoration is the product of human imagination rather than urban necessity. The end result is inevitably less familiar than the end result of necessary restoration. To some extent, cosmetic restoration must always be a work of human imagination, and it is, therefore, far more revealing.

There is no doubt, of course, that the fumes of passing cars and the airborne chemical gunk of the modern age are eating away at the fabric of the Eternal City. In Rome, oil-fired central heating is a particular problem. Atmospheric pollution is the latest in a long line of enemies that Rome's monuments have had to withstand; barbarians at the gate, angry Germans, sacking Spaniards, imperial troops, English souvenir hunters, Napoleon, greedy popes, liberating Americans: they have all done their bit to ruin Rome's ruins and to make necessary the true restoration that has taken place at irregular intervals since the death of Nero. The Roman populace itself has contributed mightily to the civic despoliation. In Julius II's time the lazy Romans were still burning the stones of their ancient past in order to make cheap building lime: today they are zooming around in pestilent vehicles that disgorge ruin-munching gases. But there is more to all this manic restitution than the city's physical need of repair. Nobody has yet suggested that unless the Sistine Chapel was restored in the eighties it would have fallen down. That was simply not the case. All over Italy a comprehensive restoration of the country's glorious past was being embarked upon for reasons that were as aesthetic as they were practical. Restitution was in the air; restoration was à la mode.

The four bronze horses of San Marco have dominated the skyline of Venice since 1204. Originally looted from Constantinople, they quickly became a symbol of the eternal power and pride of the Serenissima. Before the advent of the restoration boom, these horses of San Marco had left Italy only once, and that was in 1797, when the victorious Napoleon carried them off to Paris. It was an Italian typewriter company, Olivetti, that finally succeeded in forcing them to leave Italy a second time. Olivetti financed the restoration of the four great horses, and, as part of the deal, the finest of the proud bronze beasts was sent on a long promotional tour of some of the world's leading typewriter markets (we were still living in the precomputer age at the time). The same typewriter giants went one better with the magnificent crucifix of Cimabue. Since it had been installed in the church of Santa Croce at the end of the thirteenth century, Cimabue's *Crucifix* had never left the confines of Florence. Gravely damaged during the Arno flood of 1966, it was duly restored and then lugged around the globe in a curious, postrestoration state—part original artwork, part masterpiece of modern science. The worst of the damaged patches were disguised by pointillist infills whose exact color composition had apparently been worked out by a computer. Cimabue's *Crucifix* had become a thirteenth-century–twentieth-century hybrid.

It was a crucial change in Italy's fiscal laws, promising tax concessions to those who sponsored restoration, that triggered the restitution boom of the 1980s. In Milan, Leonardo's *Last Supper* was being restored, again (with disastrous consequences). So was Masaccio's Brancacci Chapel in Florence, where Michelangelo and the breaker of his nose, Torrigiani, had gone to learn drawing. Rome was in competition with Florence, Florence was in competition with Venice, Venice was in competition with Milan. On various economic, political, and cultural fronts, Italy was experiencing a second renaissance.

In Bologna, in the restoration of a disrupted fifteenth-century sculptural group known as *Il Compianto,* The Lamentation, the exact orientation of the individual sculptures of Christ and the six grieving figures around him was re-created with the help of a computer that could actually determine their proper positions by analyzing each statue's facial expressions and body language.

In Venice, in the year when the famous Biennale was devoted to science and technology, Veronese's *Feast at the House of Levi* became the focus of a major restoration exhibition. Wider than a London double-decker bus, packed with even more incident, this controversial Veronese painting had led to the painter's being summoned by the Inquisition to defend his inclusion of "buffoons, drunkards, Germans, dwarfs, and other such scurrilities" in what was originally intended to be a Last Supper.

Veronese explained his biblical irreverence in a famous speech: "We painters assume the same license as do poets and madmen." Then he changed the title of the painting from *The Last Supper* to *Feast at the House of Levi.* During the exhibition, you could hardly see the Germans, dwarfs, and other scurrilities because arranged around the room was a complicated array of computers and television screens that bleeped and flashed and told us how much the sponsors, Olivetti again, had assisted in the restoration of Veronese's masterwork.

According to Maria Francesca Monfredini, a Milanese restoration expert questioned about the spate of building work that has turned so many of the best-known art locations of Italy into building sites, "Restoration has become a boom industry. Once a craft, restoration is now a science." I would go further than Signora Manfredi and say that once a craft, restoration has become one of the performing arts. It has stepped out of the dressing room and onto center stage. How these new Italian restorers love the spotlight! The NTV camera crew clambering about the Sistine scaffold leaving no restoration detail unfilmed were to prove perfect accomplices.

This, then, is another kind of restoration, the modern Italian kind, stylish, high-profile, undertaken for all sorts of economic, fashionable, touristic, scientific, and —sometimes—unnecessary reasons. Rome was not In Peril, as Venice was. Unlike Florence, Rome had not been flooded. This epidemic of Roman restoration broke out not because Rome was falling down but because the city's fine detailing was being blurred by acid rain and central-heating fumes. Rome was finally old and rich and vain enough to put herself in for a complete face-lift. An old tart was brightening herself up for the art tourists. The results were fascinating.

THE LETTER

In the winter of 1986–1987 a flurry of letters was dispatched from the U.S.A. to Italy on the subject of Italian restoration. One of them was the agonized epistle from fourteen notable American artists sent to Pope John Paul II asking for the cleaning of the Sistine ceiling to be suspended until all the available scientific data had been carefully reexamined. "We fully recognize the noble purpose of those who have authorized the restoration. . . . We respectfully propose a pause in the restoration, however, to allow a thorough analysis of the results obtained so far," wrote Robert Rauschenberg, James Rosenquist, Robert Motherwell, Christo, and Andy Warhol's ghost. In the same week at the beginning of March, 1987, the fourteen American artists addressed a second letter to the Italian embassy in Washington, demanding that restoration work on Leonardo da Vinci's *Last Supper* in Milan also be reconsidered.

In the case of the *Last Supper* in the refectory of Milan's S. Maria delle Grazie, the pantheon of American artists had good reason to be concerned. Ever since it was completed in the final years of the fifteenth century, Leonardo's experimental wall painting had proved itself to be every Sunday-school teacher's dream and every art restorer's nightmare. Leonardo had apparently embarked upon the *Last Supper* dissatisfied with the fragmentary nature of the traditional fresco technique. Painting in daily patches did not allow the artist to control the overall effect of the fresco to the degree that Leonardo seems to have desired. And so he evolved an ambitious new technique that involved painting in oil on a resin undercoat. Disastrously, the oil and the resin dried at different rates, and the surface of the painting began to deteriorate almost immediately. Today it is no more than a noble ruin, a universally overused icon of religiosity. In February, 1987, the most recent of a busy sequence of restorations of the *Last Supper* had to be suspended halfway across the painting when it was discovered that adequate checks on the atmospheric conditions inside the refectory had not been made. It appears there had been some quintessentially Italian disagreement between the Sovrintendente per i Monumenti and the Sovrintendente per i Beni Storiche e Artistiche as to whose jurisdiction the painting lay under. The *Last Supper* was closed to the public. Adequate atmospheric controls were instigated. But Leonardo da Vinci's masterwork has been flaking off the walls for five hundred years, and nothing the restorers do will stop its relentless metamorphosis into dust. The only place where the *Last Supper* will ever look healthy and complete is in the full-scale copy that Andy Warhol made in 1986, where he valued the painting at fifty-nine cents, the price of a *Last Supper* postcard. Olivetti, who financed this latest restoration, paid out considerably more than that in order to be clearly identified in the minds of the public with a major conservation debacle.

The controversy over the ultimately irreparable *Last Supper* has undoubtedly influenced thinking about the cleaning of the Sistine fresco, and dented confidence in it. Here, after all, were the two most influential wall-paintings of the Renaissance being restored simultaneously, and both, it seemed, were experiencing serious restoration difficulties. When the fourteen notable American Modernists sent their letter to the pope, they were expressing more than a specific worry about two notable conservation programs. The pantheon of painters was also voicing a widely felt suspicion that in the course of this current epidemic of Italian restoration, unalterable changes were being imposed upon the core fabric of the Renaissance. In this the fourteen Modernists were absolutely right.

The Vatican had no difficulty ignoring the complaints of the American artists. The chief restorer, rising up to his full intellectual height, which is considerably taller than his body height, for Signor Colalucci is a compact man in the Michelangelo mold, dismissed the letter with some confidence. "We studied the problem for years before we began," he replied to the suggestion that restoration be suspended until all the available data had been reexamined. "We would stop if we thought we were unsure of what we are doing, but we are not. So we will continue, as I fear the criticism will."

He was absolutely right in this last assumption.

In the autumn of 1986, Professor James Beck, head of art history at Columbia University, published an article in *Arts* magazine expressing his profound doubts about the Sistine restoration. According to James Beck, the Vatican cleaning was "a disaster." Beck's main argument was that while taking off the centuries of dark glue and candle smoke that had obscured the true colors of Michelangelo's fresco, the Sistine conservationists were also removing delicate glazes and final touches applied by Michelangelo at the end of the Sistine campaign. Beck followed up his article in *Arts* magazine with an open letter to the Vatican restorers, which he sent to the Italian daily *La Repubblica*. In this open letter James Beck accused Gianluigi Colalucci and his team of "indiscriminate removal of 'secco' passages and veils of tone applied by Michelangelo himself." The dramatic high spot of this open letter came when Beck demanded of Colalucci: "Will you go down as the man who destroyed the subtlety of Michelangelo's ceiling?" This rhetorical question sent a shudder through Roman pride that could be felt back in the Etruscan era.

Other critics opposed to the cleaning quickly joined in, most of them American. The restoration was "brutalising Michelangelo." The restoration was a mistake of the same magnitude as "the space shuttle disaster." Beck himself compared it to "an artistic Chernobyl."

These opposition arguments (when inspected properly through the skims of lurid similes) took two forms. The more sedate critics were worried that the removal of layers of animal glue and soot was exposing Michelangelo's fresco to modern airborne toxics of a potency that the painting had never had to face before. The thick glues might have darkened the original fresco, but at least they protected it from the worst of the atmospheric pollutants. These critics undoubtedly had a point. Four years after the Sistine lunettes were cleaned, it was already noticeable that they had darkened considerably. This prompted the Vatican scientists to insist upon the installation of central heating in the walls of the chapel. No one knows what long-term effects this central heating will have on the fresco. It is one of the axioms of art restoration that every change effected at point A will sooner or later have implications for point B.

But it was the other main line of opposition argument that precipitated the Sistine restoration onto the front pages of the world's newspapers in the summer of 1987. This was fundamentally an aesthetic argument. But it was also, at its height, an entertaining geopolitical catfight, as one generation of American scholars was put firmly in its place by another, older, generation of European experts. Professor Beck's principal argument was that the Vatican restorers were taking too much off the surface of the Sistine ceiling. To remove the thick layer of glue and soot from the fresco, the cleaners applied a solvent solution called AB 57, a revivifying cocktail described in some detail in the NTV restoration special: ammonium bicarbonate, sodium bicarbonate, the antifungal agent known as Desogen, the thixotropic agent called carboxymethylcellulose, and, if there were salt efflorescences to be cleaned away, also a saturated solution of dimethylformamide, all dissolved in distilled water. The solvent solution was applied to the fresco soaked into poultices of Japanese paper that were left on the plaster for three minutes at a time. When the poultices were removed, so were the layers of filth and glue attached to them. Also removed, according to Beck and Co., were Michelangelo's final glazes and touches, *l'ultima mano* which drew the entire composition together. When all these final touches were thrown away, the result was, said the fiercest critics of the restoration, the false Michelangelo we see before us now, a Day-Glo Michelangelo, or, as one particularly underhanded opponent put it, "a Benetton Michelangelo." According to Frank Mason, president of the newly formed International Art Preservation Society, Michelangelo's masterpiece was being cleaned "like a rug."

The Vatican was, for once, quick to answer its critics. A team of impressively respectable art conservators, drawn mostly from various American museums, was invited to study the Sistine restoration and to publish its findings. According to a very piqued Gianluigi Colalucci, Professor James Beck had stayed on the scaffold only for the length of time that Andy Warhol said a man should be allowed to be famous—fifteen minutes. The team of conservators was encouraged to study the cleaning campaign at much greater length and in greater depth. As it happened, they reported back almost immediately, enthusiastically supporting the Vatican restorers. The suggestion that Michelangelo used some sort of tinted glaze to tone down his colors and keep the fresco dark was dismissed as unlikely. Colalucci said: "It is a stupidity."

"The new freshness of the colors and the clarity of the forms on the Sistine ceiling," reported the commission, "are totally in keeping with 16th century painting and affirm the full majesty and splendor of Michelangelo's creation." The group supported the Vatican's insistence that the true color of Michelangelo frescoes had been "obscured by uneven layers of soot, glue, salt deposits and numerous previous restorations," and continued, "All these conditions combine to falsify the grandeur of Michelangelo's intention by flattening the forms and reducing the colors to a monochrome that has misled generations." In the last, nicely phrased observation, they were indubitably right.

During the swapping of these various arguments some intriguing stories began to emerge about previous Sistine restorations. The infamous Mazzuolis, father and son, had originally cleaned the frescoes between 1710 and 1713, using Greek wine as their chief cleansing agent. It was the resinous content of Greek wine that made it an ideal solvent (and still makes it undrinkable today). A previous restorer, Lagi, in 1625 had removed the dirt by scrubbing the fresco with cheap bread. If the dirt was particularly tenacious, the stale bread was moistened with water. It had all been terrifyingly hit-or-miss, and the fact that no serious long-term damage had resulted was a tribute to, and proof of, the essential soundness of Michelangelo's fresco technique.

The new Vatican restorers with their Apollo workstation carefully bleeping away had approached the cleaning of the Sistine ceiling as Michelangelo (we now know) had approached its painting, sensibly, thoroughly, logically, professionally, and with the absence of any painterly histrionics of the kind we might have described as Michelangelesque before this restoration revealed that adjective to be completely inappropriate. The application of the Sistine solvent in small poultices, the procedure that Frank Mason described as cleaning the Sistine ceiling "like a rug," was a deliberately repetitive process that would, in the words of the Vatican apologists, "guarantee the highest margin of safety and would not require either emotional involvement or complex mechanical manipulation on the part of the restorers." It was a procedure designed to take the accident out of restoration work. Given the size of the fresco, the cleaning method had to be universally applicable. Individual restorers' contributions had to be indistinguishable. It was precisely this lack of emotional involvement and human decision making in the cleaning procedure that frightened critics.

But the suggestion that Michelangelo painted his fresco in clear Renaissance colors and then deliberately darkened them by applying brown animal glues—which is essentially what the opposition camp was claiming—really was a preposterous one, particularly as the Vatican scientists had long before discovered layers of dust and dirt in between the fresco proper and the brown animal varnish on top, indicating that this varnish had been added some time later. Colalucci, drawing himself up to his full intellectual height again, asked the *Washington Post*: "How could a man of genius, a man who was master of his technique, ever have sought to dim and darken such lifelike beauty?" The critics, he continued, "are playing on a public that likes things mysterious. They don't seem to know painting a fresco is a simple but very precise technique. We know how it was done, and we are doing nothing at all to harm it."

There was never any real doubt as to who would win the cleaning argument. The Italian restorers had masses of fresco experience, entire computers full of facts, and centuries of *droit d'Européen* to call upon. The American critics had powerful gut feelings. Those gut feelings were an eye-opening guide to the tenacity of the Michelangelo myth. After all, who among us looking up for the first time at this new, bright, clear Sistine ceiling, perfectly rational, a light-filled work, was not tempted by the doubt: it can't be so? The old Charlton Heston image of Michelangelo was a powerful image indeed. And so the row over the cleaning of the Sistine ceiling was as revealing as it was, briefly, exciting. The sight of Italian art experts, used to being venerated unquestioningly by their own nationals, being forced into the witness box by brash foreigners had real theatrical frisson. Underlying the entire affair was an issue more far-reaching even than the eventual appearance of the Sistine ceiling. The cleaning rumpus was undertowed by a widely accepted assumption of how genius *ought* to look. The dark, grim, black, troubled Michelangelo who had been recognized and adored on the Sistine ceiling for half a millenium, and about whom so much prose of the deepest purple had been written, fitted this prevailing assumption much more comfortably than the bright, lucid, clear-eyed Michelangelo tantalizingly emerging from the bath of AP 57.

Entire careers had been constructed on the belief that Michelangelo was a saturnine individualistic exception to the Renaissance's norms. Having accused him of painting the "monstrous dream of a Hindu" on the vault of the Sistine Chapel, the Nobel Prize–winning Romain Rolland then looked up and discovered "a symphony of mad force which sweeps in every direction and beats against the walls." It would basically be impossible to write that sentence with any conviction today. Or to feel what the sculptor Guillaume felt when he entered the chapel and sensed "the weight of heavy entrails." Julius Meier-Graffe said that "Michelangelo hurls beauty into us." Not today he doesn't. Today he persuades us of beauty's quietude. Goethe thought he heard "a mighty crash" heralding "the coming of the Sun." That crash is inaudible now. When Bernard Berenson surveyed the Sistine ceiling and wrote, "At last appeared the man who was the pupil of nobody, the heir of everybody . . . who saw and expressed the meaning of it all," he was ignoring the existence of a fresco technician who had been taught correct Renaissance procedures in the studio of Ghirlandaio. When Sydney J. Freedberg looked up and exclaimed, "For the moment of this fresco God and Michelangelo enjoy a confusion of roles," he was underestimating Michelangelo's entirely human labor. In today's Sistine Chapel, that kind of underestimation is impossible.

The assumption that Michelangelo departed from two centuries of correct Florentine fresco procedure (as Leonardo had done with the *Last Supper*) was easily made because he was surely, according to the popular imagination, that kind of artist, wayward and willful. In fact, as the cleaning progressed, it unveiled a careful traditionalist, a master craftsman who followed accepted fresco painting techniques to the letter, who worked with assistants, and who in this clean, rational, carefully constructed composition was more of a typical Renaissance artist and less of an unpredictable genius than had ever been expected.

The restoration of the Sistine ceiling owes its origins to a pair of unarguably minor painters called Hendrick van der Broeck and Matteo da Lecce. It was while the Vatican restorers were doing routine maintenance work on two undistinguished frescoes by this undistinguished twosome that they ran various checks on Michelangelo's lunettes above and found that minute flecks of color were lifting away from the surface in several places. Immediate restoration was prescribed.

The Sistine restoration may have been prompted by particular concern over the state of particular lunettes, but it demands also to be viewed as the epicenter of a restoration epidemic. Thousands of restorers spent the eighties bringing the past up to scratch, cleaning it, fixing it, injecting it with solidifying resins, coating it with antiacids, re-carving its details, infilling its gaps with a variety of computer-generated pointillist go-anywhere paint, mea-suring it, weighing it, x-raying it, burning minute sam-ples of it to analyze its chemical composition, recording its spectroscopic reality on graphs, bombarding it with ultraviolet light, rubbing it with distilled water, from Pompeii to Palermo, from Pisa to the Pantheon, in Ar-ezzo, Urbino, Siena, Rimini, Ravenna, experts have been probing the past, photographing it, digitizing it, and exploring it sonically. In twenty years we have acquired two thousand years' worth of knowledge about the com-position of the greatest concentration of art objects in the world. For what?

The end result of this incessant probing and repair is that the past has now been more or less frozen in its tracks. What we have now is by and large what the world will always have. Future restorers may tinker with the detailing of the ceiling, remove some of the watercolor repaints added by the present cleaners, but they will never be in a position to do what today's restorers have done, to rewrite the Sistine ceiling, to reevaluate it completely. Those gorgeous, freshly revealed Sistine colors may be-come less intense—how quickly they lose that glow of newness—but, barring a real act of God, an earthquake, a war, this is how the fresco will look for the rest of its natural life. No more candles at mass pumping soot into the beard of Michelangelo's Almighty, no more braziers and incense burners obfuscating the Sistine air, no more Greek wine rubbed into the plaster, no more stale bread deposited in the cracks. What the Sistine ceiling is now, is what it will be.

Signor Colalucci was absolutely right when he complained of the public's love of mystery. He is right to say that the simple technique of fresco is not a mysterious technique. But the accidental darkness of those candles, the clumsy glue jobs of the Mazzuolis, the old fingers of Adam painted by Carnevali: these were the battle scars of a venerable masterpiece. Fairly or unfairly earned, they were the growth marks of five hundred years. In removing them we have reversed the aging process itself, turned an old masterpiece into a spring chicken again. For what?

For the tourists, certainly. Tourists rule the Vatican and began to do so when Julius II built his sculpture court in the Belvedere and thus established the first pleasure garden to be seen in Rome since antique times. The Sistine Chapel may still be the technical center of Christendom, but woe betide the foolish Christian who tries to light a holy candle in there today. The judo-trained museum guards will converge from all Vatican directions. Tourists like the past to be old and dark but not so old and dark that it cannot be seen clearly. The Vatican's enormous saving in electricity bills and light bulbs for the illumination of the new ceiling is a spared expense that millions of visitors a year will fully support.

There are twelve great seers painted on the Sistine ceiling, seven all-seeing prophets and five all-seeing sibyls, seven biblical fortune-tellers and five pagan ones, all peering at the eventual fate of the true Catholic believer. None of them could have foreseen that one day a Japanese television company specializing in quiz shows and soaps would pay for the restoration of the most celebrated masterpiece in Christian art. Who could have dreamed in Nagasaki in 1650, as Japanese Catholics were being forced to step on the face of Christ to confirm their hatred of the True Faith, that the Sistine ceiling would one day become such an unlikely symbol of the new balance of East-West power. Today in Nagasaki there is an entire theme park devoted to the arrival of the first Europeans. There are fake Great Ships in the harbor of the almost-chosen people. Sitting in a full-size re-creation of one such boat, the modern visitor to Kyushu can sample the lurch of the sixteenth-century waves—hydraulically—and the roar of the sixteenth-century oceans—in full quadraphonic sound. NTV proved to be model modern sponsors. The decorum that was maintained not only on the Sistine scaffold by Japanese photographers but also at ground level by the NTV merchandisers was welcome. The impressive dignity of the Sistine restoration owed much to an obvious, and understandable, Japanese nervousness in the presence of Christian art.

And so fate conspired to ensure that the restoration of the Sistine Chapel did not fall into the obtrusive and surrealistic category of the brightly colored plastic parcel. The thin and neat scaffolding bridge moved elegantly along the ceiling like a very slow windshield wiper. In front of it lay the old dark Michelangelo, the great tragedian, all basso profundo and crescendo. Behind it the colorful new one, a lighter touch, a more inventive mind, a higher pitch, alto and diminuendo. It was being able to see both of them at once—Beethoven turning into Mozart before your eyes—that made this restoration such a memorable piece of theater. And such a controversial event.

The antirestoration lobby—in truth, no more than a handful of enthusiastic American professors soaked to the soul in the *terribilità* myth—had no real case. Their argument that the cleaning was removing Michelangelo's final layer, *l'ultima mano,* the finishing touches he applied when the fresco was dry, was based on a sense of loss and not on sensible research. That the painter emerging from the back end of the windshield wiper should have appeared such a complete stranger was a testament not only to the number of candles burned in the Sistine Chapel but also to the corrosive power of the Michelangelo myth. This all-agony-no-ecstasy image of Michelangelo was built up on a series of misreadings. The massive Moses trapped in the double-glazing at St. Peter in Chains would have appeared less of a terrible giant to Freud, less of a projection of the ultimate parental authority, if he had finished up in the place he was intended for, high above the tomb of Julius, surrounded by scores of sculptural colleagues of the same size. If Michelangelo's Slaves had been completed as planned, instead of being abandoned in midmarble, moodily emerging . . . If the Sistine ceiling had never had candles or braziers burning in it . . . If Steve McQueen rather than Charlton Heston had played Michelangelo . . . The all-agony-no-ecstasy image of Michelangelo has been built up on a series of historical accidents.

The new Michelangelo is no longer a troubled exis-

tentialist. His ceiling is no longer such a doomy out-
pouring of religious angst. In full Renaissance color, it
stands revealed as the work of a much more rational mind.
Carefully plotted compartments of color have replaced the
all-over effusions of despair. Up on the Sistine ceiling,
pinks have replaced browns and grays. There is rather a
lot of green, bright as Opal Fruits, that draws attention
to itself. This is not the Sistine ceiling of the old art
history books, a work of miserable individualistic prognosis and thunderous personal pessimism. This is a bright,
light, colorful, and uplifting Renaissance spectacle, less
of a warning and more of a celebration. The monochrome
that misled generations is gone forever. No wonder that
in some art-historical circles its departure has been greeted
with howls of despair. What the restorers seem to have
removed from the ceiling—along with the buildup of
candle soot, the smoke from all those papal conclaves that
have been held here, the botched handiwork of previous
restorers, the Greek wine, and the old bread—is that
quality of suppressed anger and foreboding which Michelangelo's contemporaries and scholars since have called
terribilità.

Figures that had previously seemed downright scary
set deep back in their darkness now emerge solid and
integrated. The famous *ignudi* appear less acrobatic, more
relaxed. The Delphic Sibyl is prettier, less awesome. On
the NTV special that Hiroko Katayama watched in Tokyo, the microphones listening in on the stern Vatican
restorers heard one of them relax, and begin flirting with
her. "Look at that mouth. She's very sexy, isn't she?" he

asked himself. Yes, indeed, she is. Even the Almighty Himself seems a fluffier, friendlier sort of divinity, closer to the one admired but not recognized by Michelangelo's earliest biographer: "Among the most important figures is one of an old man, in the middle of the ceiling, who is represented in the act of flying through the air."

The new ceiling is thus a long, full-color critique of the tortured-genius myth. And it is not surprising that its loudest critics have been American, for it was under the fake vault of Charlton Heston's movie set that the mythical Michelangelo gave his greatest, hammiest performance.

The windshield wiper has finished its journey across the greatest painting in Western art. In my opinion, it has made that painting substantially greater by celebrating it as the work of a rational, hardworking, colorful human rather than some sweaty, impulsive, God-driven genius.

So, it's *sayonara* to the old Michelangelo. Welcome to the new.

He who from nothing made all things ordained
That time in two parts should be severed; one
He handed over to the mighty sun,
The other with the nearer moon remained.

From this event, fortune and fate sprang forth,
Mischance or happiness to each man fell.
To me was sent the dark time, I know well,
For it has always been with me since birth.

—Michelangelo
(translated by Elizabeth Jennings)

INDEX

GRATEFUL ACKNOWLEDGMENT IS MADE TO
THE FOLLOWING FOR PERMISSION TO REPRINT
COPYRIGHTED MATERIAL:

Harcourt Brace Jovanovich, Inc. and Faber and Faber Ltd.
for permission to reprint and excerpt from "The Love Song
of J. Alfred Prufrock" originally published in *Collected
Poems 1909–1962* by T.S. Eliot. Copyright © 1936 by
Harcourt Brace Jovanovich, Inc. Copyright renewed ©
1964, 1963 by T.S. Eliot. Reprinted by permission of
the publishers.

David Higham Associates Ltd. for permission to reprint
material from *The Sonnets of Michelangelo* translated by
Elizabeth Jennings. Copyright © 1988 by Carcanet Press
Ltd. Reprinted by permission of David Higham Associates
Ltd.

Oxford University Press for permission to reprint material
from *Michelangelo: Life, Letters and Poetry* translated by
George Bull and Peter Porter (World's Classics Paperback). Copyright © 1987 by George Bull. Reprinted by
permission of Oxford University Press.

Princeton University Press for permission to reprint selec-
tions from *Complete Poems and Selected Letters of Michelangelo*
translated by Creighton Gilbert. Copyright © 1980 by
Creighton Gilbert. Permission granted by Creighton
Gilbert.